IT'S NOT
JUST
ABOUT THE
WRENCHES!

THE BASICS ABOUT YOUR CAR, ITS
CARE AND WHY THE CULTURE OF
A SMALL AUTO SHOP IS SO
IMPORTANT IN BUSINESS

GREGORY A. SKOLNIK, AMAM, CMAT-L1

ISBN-10: 1-946203-16-5
ISBN-13: 978-1-946203-16-8

**Expert
Press**

www.ExpertPress.net

Table of Contents

Foreword

When Greg Skolnik asked that I write the Foreword to his book, I was delighted! With 38 years of consulting, process reengineering, and customer service improvement projects, I've been interested both personally (two Hondas under his care) and professionally in witnessing the growth and success of Motor-Works, Inc. over the past 21 years.

Here are some business truths I've discovered working with clients as diverse as huge federal data centers, mid-sized oil companies, and child-abuse shelters:

1. Human relationships are built on two things – trust and shared interests

2. All business is personal

3. Success or failure is always about the "soft tissue" issues … how humans are handled will determine the outcome of any project or business.

Time and again, I've seen perfectly good software applications fail in one business, and succeed in another – but were the users trained, did the culture get accommodated in the roll-out? The joy of being a Motor-Works Inc. client is in Greg's external as well as internal understanding of those three truths – and how he effectively manages the business, and drives its culture by the core values in which he so clearly believes.

Being a metrics-driven analyst, we've had some pointed conversations about how to handle a business problem or two – Greg's commitment to the human element was unwavering, while I will admit, I'm a bit more hard-nosed. Over the decades, it's been a renewing experience to watch him often prove me wrong!

This book will give you some clear, caring, and concise practical guidance on how to manage your vehicle so it's optimized; how to find help if it is not working; and what to know about your car so you are as educated as possible. I hope that you enjoy the book as much as I have – now I can chat knowledgeably with the wonderful staff. All of them have internalized the values that Greg champions. The excellence and attention to detail with which they tend to our cars, and care for us as customers, should serve as the standard to which all repair businesses are measured!

Nancy Lee Hutchin (ret.)
Senior Advisor, Office of the Secretary
Department of Transportation

(Nancy Lee Hutchin published 35 articles on customer service and process improvement, and was a frequent speaker at international conferences. She was President, Executive Women's Roundtable, in Washington DC ('05-'06) and is included in five Marquis *Who's Who* books: *Finance and Industry, American Women, World, Science and Engineering, and America.*)

Acknowledgements

I would like to mention two business owners without whose suggestion this book would have never been written. Mike Davidson and Michael DeLon pushed me along through this process and for that I am ever grateful.

Special thanks go to my good friend, Ben Pitkin, for the countless hours he worked helping me find the right words. I would also like to thank my niece, Shayna Skolnik for the fantastic illustrations.

I look for people to learn from every day. Jim Murphy has been an invaluable asset as a coach and has consistently demonstrated selfless care for my personal and business development. He is backed by the ethical programs and dedicated staff at Elite Worldwide. Bob Cooper, its founder, has made a successful mission to inspire thousands in this industry to be better at our craft. Thank you all.

I am (and have been) blessed to have wonderful employees. You are very much appreciated and I have learned from each and every one of you. It takes a team to make this work and you are the true superstars!

In addition, I must thank the thousands of wonderful clients who have appreciated my style of business culture for all of these years. You are the folks that help me stay the course every day.

I would like to acknowledge my parents, Ed and Anita, for instilling the right stuff to help me get to this day. Also, my brothers and sister, whom I love very much; I realize every day just how blessed I am to have good relationships with each of you.

I must mention my sons, Chris and Aaron, my daughter-in-law, Mary, as well as my wonderful grandkids: Kayleigh, Nathan,

Olivia, and Joshua. You guys are the reason I work as hard and laugh as hard as I do. I love you all…to the moon and back!

My wonderful wife, Carol has been my life partner for more than 40 years now. She has been a mentor and helped me bushwhack my way to create the spiritual path I never knew.

I have learned so much from her. She shares her perspective openly, and is my sounding board and confidant through the many tantrums and rants as well as the accolades and achievements.

 She allows me the space to be who I am and for that I am eternally grateful. Thank you for helping push me along through the book writing process as well. We have witnessed much together and she never ceases to amaze me. Carol, I love you.

Greg

Mission Statement

Motor Works, Inc. (MWI) is a business with strong ethics and principles. We always put people ahead of money. Our staff competently cares for each client in a way that results in long-term relationships.

We tirelessly focus on benefits and behaviors to support our almost four decade-long reputation as a respected, ethical and valued service provider and community supporter.

We promise mutual respect, empathy and compassion for all parties, in an atmosphere which encourages personal responsibility and opportunity for continued growth.

What You Could Learn By Reading This Book

This book has three purposes:

1. It describes how this business became this business. How the culture evolved and how the steadfast ethics of the owner have built their wonderful reputation.

2. It offers advice for folks who have already started—or dream of starting—a small business of any type.

3. It provides logical and concise information on how a car functions—and the simple things an owner can do to keep it functioning smoothly for as long as possible.

Many of my clients know some of the stories about me and the culture I have created at MWI over the years. With this book, I hope to share that experience with all readers. Perhaps some of you will recommend (or even give a copy of) this book to the folks at your own repair facility. If so, I invite you to tell them they can call me directly if they have questions. They can use the e-mail link at our website (www.motor-works.com) or contact the shop directly at 301-424-2800 and ask for Greg (that's me!).

Maybe some of you are thinking: "OK, but what made you decide to write a book about these things?" And maybe some are also thinking: "What makes you think *your* insights on cars and small business are so special?" And maybe a handful of you are now thinking, "Yeah! What makes *you* so special, Greg?" Well, I have the type of brain that is wired pretty well for what I do. I am methodical, with an inquisitive streak. Like a three-year-old, I am always asking *"why"* …as in, "why is this happening? Why does this mechanism do that? Why is…" well…you get the idea.

Quite *unlike* a three-year-old, however, I have decades of experience to draw upon. I have acquired a vast knowledge base over the years, and that will enable me to deliver what I believe to be pertinent information designed to help you gain a better understanding of your vehicle and its care, and to ensure you squeeze every mile out of your maintenance and repair dollar.

More importantly, I understand that each reader is an amazing soul, blessed with interests, skills, and natural talents that I could only dream about. I respect each and every one of you.

We each have talents, interests, and skills that we have developed and honed over time. This observation brings my dentist to mind. He and I are not only on a first-name basis with each other, I think I was one of his first patients. I have no intention of finding another dentist. While I have a cursory understanding of what he is doing (and why) when he's at work on my teeth, I would NEVER attempt to do that myself. Would you? I didn't think so.

I'm also amazed that the 80 plus-year-old barber who still cuts my hair knows all about me. I suppose I could save a few bucks by standing in front of a mirror with a Flowbee®, but… uh…no way.

A small percentage of the vehicle-owning population are the do-it-yourselfers (DIYs) who enjoy working on their vehicles themselves, whether for sheer enjoyment or for financial necessity. I salute all of them. For the rest of the vehicle owners, we provide a service that fills a very important need in modern society. At MWI, we partner with each of our clients. We offer them peace of mind by providing logical and ethical care of their vehicle. In short, we provide skills and service that the client either can't or isn't willing to do on his or her own. This is valuable to the client. We're problem solvers.

While our role has changed a bit over the years along with automotive technology, we'll always be needed in some fashion, even after the internal combustion engine has been retired.

We consider this a crucial responsibility and we treat it accordingly. Our clients routinely refer to us as "family" or swear they will only purchase Honda- or Toyota-built cars (because that's all we work on).

That being said, my focus is on treating employees and clients in an ethical way while delivering basic understanding of how this rolling phone booth-texting station-concert hall-dining room table-urban assault vehicle-Swiss army knife of a family tool actually works. Who knows? You might pick up a few pointers. Stay alert!

Earlier, I listed this book's three purposes. Well, I was holding out on you. There's really a fourth purpose, too. My approach to auto repair and to being a small businessman is informed by a philosophy of building mutually constructive relationships and fostering trust. I extend that philosophy to all of my personal interactions, not just the commercial ones. I also believe my track record proves that treating all people decently and respectfully is *not* contrary to business success; rather, it's the *cornerstone* of business success. The words contained within these pages are intended to help others, in some small way, to improve someone else's life, to give back. That is one of my core values.

Again, please don't hesitate to check out more information on our website (www.motor-works.com) or contact the shop directly at 301-424-2800.

—Greg

IT'S NOT
JUST ABOUT THE
WRENCHES!

Clients

They are the reason we do what we do. We enjoy the wonderful relationships we create, one-on-one…day-by-day with each client. We will never take them for granted.

It is important that the reader understand how the satisfied clients chose their shop and why they stay with their service provider. MWI has enjoyed a steady stream of testimonials, thank-you notes, letters, emails, and online reviews for decades. Expedience requires they be pared down although you can read many, many more online at www.motor-works.com; or in our office, where a large binder of testimonials lives. An abbreviated list of snippets includes:

- *Fair, reliable and consistent.*

- *I appreciate their communication skills*

- *Peace of mind driving*

- *They're like extended family*

- *We are impressed*

- *Honest service*

- *Recommend without reservation*

- *Top notch approach to customer satisfaction*

- *Friendly and professional*

- *Only the best*

- *You guys are the BOMB!*

- *In and out in under 90 minutes*

- *Reliable, cost effective, honest and nice*

- *Makes a lot of sense*

- *Like family – only better!*

- *Others are fighting hard for second place*

- *Not sure what would happen without you*

If there is a pattern in the words from these actual clients, it has to do mostly with their perception of the personal treatment they experience. There are no mentions of price. That's because, while price is a consideration, it will be worth the cost if the shop can consistently provide what the client needs. That need is *to feel cared for*. There really is something to that old TV series "*Cheers*". People DO want to go where everybody knows their name. Here are testimonials from several long-term clients. I appreciate each and every one of you and thank you for your kind words.

MARY LOIS GANNON-MILLER – *Motor Works has been taking care of my cars for almost 1 million miles–that's 4 cars during the last 20+ years. The staff and technicians are knowledgeable, highly trained, courteous, always respectful and professional. The work they perform is spot on, priced fairly and done right the first time. Honestly, if Tom and Ray (of Car Talk fame) had their garage in Rockville it would be called Motor Works.*

JANET SAROS – *A friend called me recently to say she had test-driven a Subaru and really liked it. She then noted that I wouldn't be interested since I was so loyal to Hondas. The truth of the matter is that it isn't the carmaker that commands my loyalty – it's my mechanics. I have taken my cars to Motor Works for over 30 years and I cannot imagine going anywhere else for car maintenance. The staff at Motor Works is the epitome of professional integrity. When they say something needs to be fixed, I know it's true. When they say* they are monitoring the wear of my brakes, I know they are. They care about making my 2000 Odyssey and 2005 CRV last as long as possible and about my safety when I'm driving the cars. I trust them completely.

DR. LOUIS SOLOMON – *In this modern world there are two things that are critical to our enjoyment of living: good medical attention for physical bodies and outstanding dependable attention and care of our automobiles. Motor Works, a small automobile service company located in Rockville MD, owned and managed by the founder, Greg Skolnik takes care of the automobiles.*

I have been a steady customer for over 20 years. They have handled Hondas owned by me, my family, and my friends all that time. Their service is flawless, fairly priced, and prompt. They have a very unusual work week: their staff, which as far as I can recall has no turnovers, works 40 hours a week but in just four days: Monday-Thursday. If you have an emergency on Friday-Sunday, you have only to call the Emergency Number and your problems will be adroitly and rapidly handled. One excellent measure of a company is the devotion of their customers. Motor Works customers have essentially no turnover except through death or they foolishly move away.

A point should be made why Motor Works has been so successful. Skolnik is interested in two things: his dedicated and well trained staff and his customers. The staff members have no turnover as far as I can see. Once someone comes to work at Motor Works, and they technically measure up to Greg's high standards, they stay. They are well paid, and they work four days a week. They are part of the solution to the customer's problems. The customers are fairly and rapidly handled. The problems are always solved; the price for the service is always fair and reasonable. Mr. Skolnik has created a model of how all companies should be run. For those who are thinking of creating their own companies, regardless of the field of endeavor, emulating the procedures used by Skolnik will guarantee success.

In the past several years I have had to obtain new cars. My primary and virtually only criteria are that they be either Hondas or Toyotas. The reason for this is that these are the only automobiles that Motor Works services.

Like any other citizen of the world today, I have issues and problems: but, worrying about virtually the only method for transportation which is available to me is in the hands of Motor Works, and I have never been unhappy with their service. I highly recommend them to all Honda and Toyota owners.

Dr. William McGarvey – *I have been a customer of Motor Works since 1986. They have always been fair, reliable, consistent in their performance, and exceedingly friendly to everyone who visits them. While some may find them a bit pricey, I have not – indeed, I've gotten the benefit of many of their informal discounts. As long as I own a Honda and live in the Washington, DC region, there will only be one place for my car's upkeep – Motor Works.*

History

The Early Years

By "history," I mean my story. I will try to keep it only to the parts that might enlighten or entertain.

Every story has a beginning. In my case, it starts under a car. Are you surprised?

The youngest of four kids, two, seven and nine years older, I was born into a loving family with modest means. My father was incredibly smart and capable; my mother was funny, caring and hardworking. I was fortunate to experience their encouragement. Looking through old photographs it becomes immediately apparent that they didn't have much in the way of money, yet I never felt that we were wanting for anything. Both of them worked outside the home: my mother as a psychiatric clinic administrator at Walter Reed Army Medical Hospital in Washington DC and my father as an engineer for a NASA contractor at the Goddard Space Center in Greenbelt, Maryland.

My interest in car repair, upon recollection, was born of necessity, not as a hobby. I was one of those kids who took to wheels like a duck to water. I was intrigued and fascinated by machines and how they worked.

School & Auto Shop Class

In high school, I loved playing music and developed my peace-nik-era disdain for authority. I excelled in subjects I was interested in and had no use for others. My grades suffered. At our high school, there was no designated space for auto shop class. We were assigned a second-floor classroom at the back of the school. Mr. Snider, our instructor, loved Volkswagens and taught how to the remove the engine from a VW outside, on a patio behind school, from which two of the students could carry the engine up the stairs to the classroom. There, we were taught the basics of engine design, construction, and repair. We also worked on lawn mowers and outboard boat motors. It wasn't until years after my graduation that a proper shop was built at the school, along with a theater.

While we were still in high school, a friend of mine named Jim was hell-bent on building a VW-based dune buggy and I agreed to assist him. He had completed most of the frame and body installation. I was enlisted to help with engine work and electrical wiring. Cars like this were crude and loud and lots of fun. We both had a great time with this project. I often wonder what became of the car…I have lost touch (Sigh).

Advanced Training

One day, I received a telephone call from a representative from Lincoln Technical Institute (LTI), a top-flight automotive technical college. To this day, I am unsure of how (and by whom) the levers were pulled on my behalf in order to make this happen. In any event, my father and I visited the school and I came away having to continually push my jaw closed. I was in love with the technology and training that would have access to and the skills I would learn. My parents helped me financially and I enrolled in the program full time. It was here that I received my foundational rounding. I learned more of the physics behind electrical theory, and of hydraulics, chemistry, and stoichiometry (the science of the by-products of the combustion process). I was amazed at the complexity of modern automatic transmissions and engine design. I excelled at LTI and became one of the youngest graduates of their automotive-technology degree program.

First Employer: The Dealership Debacle

After graduation from LTI, I was offered a job at a local Ford dealership's service department. I was one of those kids with stars in his eyes for a new career. A few of those stars abruptly disappeared when I was hired at a mere $2 per hour. "Oh, that pay rate is only for a week," I was told. I would be apprenticing with an older mechanic and I was to take his "book" (meaning his workload) over time. In this job, I learned how important personal integrity is. I kept checking in with my service manager about my progress and was assured I was doing just fine. Weekly, he would say that the pay increases were being held up a bit by "corporate," but were forthcoming. I grew suspicious. During this time, I was tasked with many warranty and recall functions that were generally not simple operations, and I completed them independently without problems. Finally, after six weeks, I had to put my foot down. I had an obligation to repay my student debt, and by now I was sure I was being taken advantage of at two bucks per hour. This place was chewing through new recruits at a rapid pace. I had to find an alternative.

The VW Shop

"I don't want any damn helpers", said the older man as I stood in front of him, noticing his greasy, dirty white shirt and hands. Gone were the clean floors, painted walls, and organizational structure of the dealership service department. In this man's shop, grease, parts, and dirt were everywhere. His glasses were smudged and the telltale chalky residue on his lips betrayed the continuous ingestion of antacid.

The Ford dealership had given me a wakeup slap. Most of the stars that had been in my eyes on graduation day had now vanished behind the thick clouds of reality. I was awakening to the real world.

I finally put my self-worth in front and left that job after being lied to—over and over. I was now unemployed, and standing in front of a guy calling me a *helper*. "Sir, I'm not just a helper. You'll see that when you give me a chance." The boldness of my comeback stopped him. His eyes scanned me up and down for what seemed like an eternity and then, his demeanor lightened. He agreed to let me try.

Two German mechanics owned this VW garage and I had a strange fascination with the shop. I was intrigued by the technical aspects of Volkswagens since helping my friend Jim with his dune buggy and from working on these ingenious cars in the second-floor "shop" classroom at my high school. After all: Volkswagen engines were the only ones that two high school kids could carry up the stairs to disassemble and repair!

A portrait of the author as a young man

Over the next five years at the VW shop, I sponged knowledge from every car I worked on, every moment. I became quite proficient at my craft and elevated myself from the shop's *Chico* to their number-one technician. Chico was the name given to me by a Brazilian mechanic who worked at the shop. The name meant "newbie" or "go-fer".

I became more emboldened as time progressed and tried to hold my employers to task when I saw something they were doing that wasn't proper. Spirited arguments were becoming a weekly occurrence because of our differing ethical and technical philosophies, as well as our individual heritage and backgrounds.

These men, products of their upbringing during and after World War II, still believed they were superior to most others and their taunting message "close your eyes, Greg, and see what you really have" (nothing— get it?) still rings in my memory. I was considered second class to them. They taught me to say *"Ich bin ein hunde mensch."* I found out later this roughly means *"I am your dog-man."* I remember their laughter.

I was appalled at the callousness they exhibited in all their relationships, both within and outside the business. Between the walls of this small, dingy garage, I learned precisely how NOT to treat people.

I started to believe that I could not be a part of an organization that would allow the business behaviors and poor ethics that I was witnessing. Angry customer interactions and arguments were becoming an almost daily occurrence. I felt bad for our customers and didn't blame them in the least for their anger. One day I sat outside the shop after hours with a customer and listened to him complain. I realized that I could no longer apologize for the owners' insensitivity and lack of business scruples.

I had approached the owners with suggestions on ways to handle customers. My ideas not only went unheeded, they were disrespected. The owners' motivation was financial, and that was it.

One day, one of our customers came in and asked, on behalf of his son, if there were any job openings at the shop. Having recently fired an older mechanic for ethical "liberties," the boss agreed to hire the young man, Dan, as a helper. In a short time, Dan was enjoying learning to be a mechanic, and he became quite good. We shared a philosophy of treating customers, employees, and—well, everyone—decently, and we swiftly became great friends.

Over time, Dan and I started talking about the possibility of opening our own business. Although by now I had six years of experience as a professional mechanic, I felt so green, so unaware, and so naïve about "business". I was also so cautious (read: scared) that I wasn't sure I would take the chance if it did arise. By this time, I had married Carol, had become a father to Chris and Aaron and had a mortgage on our house to pay. It would be truly sink or swim. Our drive, technical skills, and knowledge were all we had.

Neither of us felt good about the way the shop was run or how we were treated there. As our plans gradually took shape, the every-day indignities at the VW shop piled up. Finally, we were no longer able to stand the toxic environment that

MWI's building under construction in 1979

we worked in. Dan and I took the plunge. In 1979, Motor Works was born. (More details on this later, in the "Business" chapter.)

Four Years Later

Sitting on a curb outside our very own shop after a long summer's work day, the sunlight mellowing in the reflection on the building's block facade, Dan and I had that "what next" moment. We had gotten through the start-up phase and had stabilized; figuratively, we were rolling down the sidewalk without any training wheels now, and the evidence that we were actually "doing it" was all around. In hindsight, which is almost always 20/20, I believe this was the point at which our partnership began a long, slow separation of paths.

By 1989, we had realized that the growth part wasn't so easy. Managing a partnership had become quite a chore by itself. I was more and more stressed each day. Being an Owner still chafed like an ill-fitting suit. The realization that I couldn't be an employee's *buddy* and *boss* at the same time bothered me. Meanwhile, I started seeking guidance in the legal and accounting worlds for ways to legitimize and protect the business partnership Dan and I had built and the investments we had made. While things seemed to go well as partnership relationships go, after time, we began to grow apart. Dan was very good at working on the cars although he wasn't very keen on learning about the business side of things. Tensions within our 50/50 partnership began to appear.

Going It Alone

In 1993, after three years of development, a buy-sell agreement was still only in draft form. Thousands had been spent in legal fees. The harder I pushed to finalize it, the more Dan seemed to resist. During one visit to a law office, I finally realized I had to close the book firmly on our partnership. Dan was no longer a "partner." He was an employee; a mechanic—albeit a very good one, and one who had taken the same exact dollar amount as me in salary. I felt I was taking the lion's share of the business-development responsibility on my shoulders. I was suffering severe stress by this point. After difficult negotiations, we signed the papers in June of that year. I now owned MWI myself.

Wrenches to Spreadsheets – Shaping the Business Culture

Although I offer candid judgments about the situations I faced early in my career, I believe that I have learned and grown enough to hold no lingering negativity about them. I *needed* those experiences, however uncomfortable they were at the time, to shape who I am today, and the business culture that I eventually fostered. I actually appreciate the treatment I received at those shops and with those people because, without them, I would have nothing with which to compare and contrast myself.

My enduring concern and respect for employees, both emotionally and financially, can be traced to my own early work experience. My focus on ethical treatment of clients is also a direct result of events I witnessed prior to founding MWI.

I have always continued my education. I read continuously, think about ways to improve things all the time, and ask questions; and in so doing, I generally skirt the edges of being a pain in the neck to all around.

I have attended more seminars and automotive courses than I can count, and continue to challenge myself daily. I not only participate in the *Pro Service* peer management group sponsored by Elite Worldwide (an outstanding auto repair shop management training service); I also coach other business owners across North America. I learn a lot from coaching too. When reviewing and teaching others, I am afforded a wonderful opportunity to see my own rust, so to speak.

A Major Shift – The Story of Harold T

In the early 80's, we had an older client who liked us to call him "Harold T".

Some words that might describe this man are: *charming, smart, gregarious, friendly,* and *meticulous.* He was also opinionated, and  at times, a curmudgeon. He owned a pristine VW Beetle. As a World War II veteran, he freely offered rants of vitriol for the wartime Germans even while simultaneously loving his little car from Wolfsburg.

He was a regular. I believe he enjoyed the stimulating conversations that took place as we performed some menial task on the Bug. I suspect that sometimes; Harold T would create reasons to bring his car in. Once he asked us to remove the turn signal light assemblies atop the front fenders so he could wax the painted surfaces beneath them. See what I mean?

One day, I became aware that we hadn't seen him for a while. The next week we wondered what was going on with him. The following week, I called to ask about him. His son answered the phone and informed me that Harold T was in hospice with terminal brain cancer. Although the son told me that Harold likely wouldn't recognize me, I insisted that I visit the next day.

At 8:12 that following morning, his son was on the telephone telling me that Harold T had passed away the night before. He told me of the funeral arrangements scheduled for the next day. This would be the first client funeral I ever went to. (I have lost count of how many I have attended since then. But I do keep a list of their names as well as fond memories of the relationships I had with them all.)

The day of Harold's service was very busy at MWI but I was able to open a space in the schedule so I could attend the mid-day service. I arrived late and the service had already started. I took a seat in the back row. I saw no familiar faces, nor did I know the man at the front who was eulogizing and chronicling Harold T's life. Still in my work uniform, I felt out of place, almost intruding on the family's right to a respectful goodbye. As the eulogy progressed, I was surprised as the Officiant suddenly started to describe Harold T's relationship with his *mechanic*. Like walking under an invisible waterfall, a wave of emotion flowed from my head through my core and down to my toes. The story and apparent admiration Harold had for me continued for five torturous minutes. *"I don't deserve this; I'm just his mechanic,"* I thought. The fact that his family communicated this at his funeral was an honor I wasn't prepared to receive, and yet, there it was. Heads nodded during the stories of his garage exploits. How did *they* know these stories? Had someone been watching from some hidden vantage point? Well, no, of course not—obviously, Harold had shared these stories with his family, and so had revealed how much the experiences had meant to him. Until that moment, it had never occurred to me how important my relationship was to that ONE man. This realization changed my life forever. I could not prevent the tears from streaming.

Understanding how important we are in the lives of our clients had now become part of the foundation of the business culture we enjoy today. This awareness is crucial and I routinely walk through the shop asking the staff the name of the car's owner they are working on. They must understand they are caring for a person…by caring for his or her car. This is a key distinction that differentiates Motor Works from most other businesses.

Loss

It was October, 27, 2003, a Monday. My wife, Carol, and I had just arrived for a much-needed vacation in Tucson, AZ. Early that morning, I received a call from our shop manager…his voice cracked and shook. I sat back on the sofa with my eyes wide and my hand on my head.

Russell, a certified technician and beloved member of our Motor Works team since 1997, had been involved in a head-on collision on his way to work.

A young driver had lost control of his truck and crossed the centerline, hitting Russ' Honda Civic head-on. The Civic's airbags deployed, but Russ sustained severe head trauma and was pronounced dead at the scene. The other driver was physically unhurt.

Russell

The sudden pain in my gut was followed by a wave of disbelief. I took one of those breaths…the ones that end in a heavy sigh. I felt my shoulders drop as my gaze sank to the floor. The memories flooded by, like a slideshow. I felt the welling of tears.

I flew back to Maryland to tend to my crew and attend the funeral. Other than the Officiant, I was the only person to speak at his funeral. I struggled through my prepared notes, pausing over and over to choke back the emotion. It was a rough day. We were a family, and we had lost a beloved and devoted member.

In addition to the hurt we felt personally, the shock to the business was huge. I had neither prepared nor planned for something like this. We all pulled closer together and acknowledged our losses. I hired a grief counsellor who helped us as we all worked through our grief differently. We carried on.

John

Little did we know that just over three years later, we would be revisiting this hell with the tragic loss of a second team member, John. Still raw from the loss of Russ, the team would again be tested in its ability to band together and work through tragedy. The thought of closing the business was fleeting, although strangely attractive as I struggled with the weight of the losses. As owner, I take the welfare of my employees personally. The pain is real. I thought, "I can't go through this again."

Russ and John remain with us today, in spirit. Their memories remind us just how important each day is and how blessed we are to have experienced their energies. This gratitude extends to all the relationships we enjoy with each other, our clients, and our business associates.

Business

Just Getting Started or Been Doing It for Some Time?

If you are planning on opening a business, wonderful! If you're already in a business and want to improve, here is a little advice from my own experiences:

- Mission–Get your mission clarified. Why do you go to work every day? Create the mission statement and post it prominently where you can see it constantly.

- Ethics – Never put money ahead of people. NEVER! Your honor is incredibly valuable to you and it's so easy to lose. Use the golden rule every day.

- Goal setting – this is a consistent challenge for me. Creating clear and concise goals for short, mid and the long term is important to ensure you have a path to get where you want to go. Think of it as a map; you are in Chicago and you want to go to New York. Without a map and compass, you'll likely never get there. Worse than that would be trying to find the way from Chicago to New York looking at a map of California.

- Funding–If you think you have enough money to start a business, you'll likely need at least twice that amount.

- Finances–Get control of the finances. Take some basic

accounting and bookkeeping courses. Learn computer tracking programs such as QuickBooks and commit to using them religiously. Understand where the dollars come from and where every penny is spent. NEVER mix your personal finances with your business…it's just not worth it. Lastly, find a great accountant. One that can speak in a language that you can comprehend. They can educate you. Don't be looking for the cheapest one. You really need to know this stuff. No kidding.

- Speed Bumps–Be prepared to deal with what appear to be insurmountable problems. They're not. Break them into little pieces and tackle them methodically and with perseverance.

- Read – Yes… there are thousands of books on business and there will be nuggets in each one that will help mold you into a savvy entrepreneur and business owner.

- Ask Why–Just like becoming a technician, I had to learn to be a business person and an employer a step at a time. Remember that we don't stop learning when we receive a diploma. Just keep going.

- Training–In the last decade, I've expanded my own training by becoming a Business Development Coach for other business owners in the automotive industry. The way I see it, in order for me to teach somebody something, I need to know it myself. Coaching encourages me to improve myself while at the same time, giving back to an industry that I love by helping other owners and managers improve their own shops. Ultimately, my knowledge not only helps the other shop owner, it also improves the working conditions for their technicians and staff members who in turn, improve the service experience for thousands of their clientele. Consider hiring a business development coach to help keep you accountable for the business improvement. I happen to work with Elite Worldwide (www.eliteworldwide.com). Based on the testimonials on their website, the expense is definitely worth it. There are many other companies nationally that offer coaching services as well. Interview and find one that you can work with…that you can build a trust relationship.

- Marketing – similarly, I never thought much about Marketing and promotion until the 90's. We've come quite a long way, especially with the importance of that thing they call the Internet. I've learned huge amounts and there's even more that I need to. The struggle continues. One thing is for sure… when you don't advertise, nothing happens that is good for the business. It must be consistent, even when you're swamped with work.

- HR – I never thought I'd have to become a Human Resources person until I learned all the things I'm not doing right. Learn the skill of hiring the right people with the right attitudes. Learn the art of delegation and become a skilled and respectful Supervisor. Learn how to clarify the employee's position statements and seek agreement on the metrics to determine when they've succeeded. You must hold them accountable for their performance. Tough to do but ultimately it helps them to grow.

Why Caring for Cars and The *Business* of Caring for Cars Are Totally Different

When you ask a small-business owner about the toughest part of being an entrepreneur, he or she will almost always tell you that it's the *business* part—meaning the administrative and paperwork side of things. It's budgeting, payroll, procurement, taxes, hiring, insurance—those and the myriad other things that we are responsible for in addition to the actual day-to-day operations of auto repair, or dog shampooing, or serving breakfast at a diner, or whatever business you're in, that we never anticipated beforehand.

Okay, by now you know that I love cars and machines in general. What you may not know is that when I decided to start the business, I had no idea how to do it...*business*, I mean. Each new task was being done for the first time, like interacting with property managers, signing leases, navigating the permitting nightmares, and—marketing? What was *that?*

This was all just at the beginning. Oh yeah, did I mention that we had only $90 in the bank on the day we opened? I believe it is true what they say, that most people go into business underfunded. I know we certainly did. We didn't have much of a plan. We didn't have contingencies: there was no 'plan B' and of course, we never even considered an exit strategy. Looking back, from more than 37 years later, I wish I knew then what I have since learned from the school of hard knocks. I know, that's hardly an original thought. There's a reason it's so widely known and repeated!

Even as I became overwhelmed by the avalanche of these issues getting started and rolling forward, I had no clue that it would get even tougher. Why, you ask? Well, for a business like this to survive, it needs to have a support staff. Team members, associates, whatever you call them, they are all employees. The big difference between being an employee and being an employer is that I had to become the BOSS. This was much harder for me than I thought it was going to be. It continues to be challenging to this day.

The Owner's Job Description

After years of training, the continual self-evaluations and the unfortunate hard-knock school lessons, I have found that the Owner's job description isn't to be both the *Head Cook and Bottle Washer*... it is much simpler, and yet so much more challenging at times.

Bob Cooper of Elite Worldwide helped me by breaking these responsibilities down into a concise list. I have learned that the business owner has five main responsibilities:

1. Set the goals for the company, both short and long-term.

2. Develop a plan to accomplish these goals.

3. Hire the best people out there.

4. Bring out the best in all that you come into contact with.

5. Assure the success of the company.

Whether you are an existing business owner or if you're thinking of starting out, I would advise you to keep these objectives in mind when you interact with customers and employees. Use this list to help guide your decision-making process. As long as your decision aligns with the goals and mission you are aiming for, you will be okay.

What MWI and Your Dentist Have in Common

Seems like a strange pairing, right? Well, here is my reasoning. First of all, I believe it would be safe to say that not too many people look forward to bringing their car in for routine mainte-nance and nobody really likes having major repairs done.

This is pretty much true for going to the dentist, right? We might not like to, and we go because we know we need to.

Good dentists are totally focused on preventive care. So is MWI.

Good dentists do a great job of educating their patients. MWI continually works to find and improve educational oppor-tunities for our clients.

Dentists do a wonderful job of pre-scheduling their patient's next appointment. Likewise, MWI has been pre-scheduling clients' appointments for decades.

Dentists do a good job of reminding their patients about their upcoming appointment. MWI has pioneered tools and systems to simplify this process, such as our appointment "e-minders." Hopefully your service provider has a similar system as well.

I'm reminded of the story of a young dental patient who complained to his dentist about having to brush his teeth all the time. The dentist replied, *"Don't worry, you only have to brush the ones you want to keep."*

Why It Is Important to Have a Well-Balanced Life

This is one of my core values. Auto repair is the type of business that can burn people out in rapid succession. (Without a doubt, it's not the only one!) This being said, I believe the key to having a solid business is having solid employees and systems that work. Part of having solid employees is in not only taking care of them, but in educating them to take better care of themselves as well. I suggest a work-hard, play-hard arrangement.

Balance is important to *me* because I don't want to be the *richest guy in the graveyard.* Get it? Good.

Why MWI Has a 4-Day Work Week

Somewhere back in 1990, I started thinking about efficiency in scheduling and decided to try an experiment. We would compress 5 days of work into 4, and then take every Friday off. It seems to have worked very well over the years; besides, it fits right in with my philosophy of balance.

In fact, maintaining balance is the primary reason I have kept this work schedule for the staff. I won't treat anyone like a machine. They deserve better. As I mentioned above, the auto service industry can burn workers out pretty quickly. In order to help my employees, I ask them to simply do something each Friday that is good for *them*… it might be relaxing, exercising, getting a massage, or riding a motorcycle…whatever… just *not working on cars professionally*. Without exception, they all value this philosophy. Wouldn't you?

Yes, some business owners think I'm totally crazy and that I am leaving quite a bit on the table in unearned profits. I'm okay with that. Another of my core values is that *I will never put money over people…ever*. A good friend and associate of mine once told me, *"The only thing that walks back from the grave is your* CHARACTER.*"* Okay, and maybe a zombie, but that's really not relevant here.

Where Is This All Going in the Future?

Sure, some esteemed futurists (like *The Jetsons*) promised us we'd have flying cars by now. That's still some ways off, I suppose.

Still, the level of technology in vehicles these days is astounding. There have been huge advances in electronics, sensors, driver aids, production techniques, materials handling, etc. The cars are designed on a computer first, which is more efficient than the old creation-by-committee process that was the standard before the advent of computer aided design.

Computers Cause Homogenized Design Similarities

There are some downsides to all of this development, however. Since most of the manufacturers are shooting for the same targets, such as more interior space, lower fuel consumption, less aerodynamic drag, and lower production costs (meaning increased profits), many late-model cars are looking more and more similar. I suppose that's to be expected, since the computer aided design is dealing with the same parameters whether it's a Honda or a Hyundai, a Lexus or a Lotus.

At first, I thought it was me. I was having more and more trouble identifying the brand of car. They were all looking so similar.

The manufacturers know this too. They are struggling to differentiate *their box* from the *other guy's box* when they all look pretty much the same to a consumer.

"Why should I buy your car over another manufacturer's car," you ask? That's a pretty straightforward question. The answers are a little harder to provide.

The automakers spend millions each year on advertising that is supposed to sway our perception of their brand. They also work hard to improve and maintain their reputation in the mind of the consumer.

Future: Less Maintenance?

One recent trend that bugs the heck out of me is the *cost-to-own* hype. While it is true that modern cars are better and more reliable, each year it seems the automakers are recommending more infrequent maintenance be performed, primarily to manipulate the *perception* that their car will be the cheapest to own. That's one way to differentiate their box from the others, right?

WRONG. All this does is devalue each car and cause us all to have to buy new cars sooner than we otherwise would. It's like a chemical that was put in our drink that makes us thirstier. We drink it to quench a thirst only to need more and more. (Why do you think many bars provide salted peanuts for free? See, it doesn't even take a sneaky chemical.)

While there have been articles touting the 10,000-mile (and longer) intervals between oil changes on modern cars, we at MWI cannot agree with the manufacturers on this one. There is empirical evidence released by the manufacturers themselves. These range from the form of service bulletins directing dealership personnel to instruct the customer that they may have to add engine oil between service stops, to warranty extensions that highlight increased engine problems and oil consumption. These conditions are a DIRECT result of the long oil change intervals suggested by the on-board maintenance minder systems, in my opinion. We counsel that there is more to servicing your car than changing the oil. In my opinion (and that of many, many others), to follow the manufacturer's service-schedule recommendation to the letter may prove penny-wise and pound-foolish. Servicing the car properly becomes a rather inexpensive form of insurance. If you plan on keeping your car for more than 12 years (and you probably should—more on that later), get on a maintenance program and stick with it. It is by far the least expensive lifetime vehicle ownership plan there is.

Future: Qualified Technicians?

There's another long-term business health problem that has been growing for decades. There are fewer and fewer qualified technicians coming into this industry. It has always been hard to find and keep qualified people; it's only become harder and harder in recent years. I have observed that our  educational system has systemically steered young people toward other sectors such as the I.T. world. This industry isn't a flashy place to work. It's also not particularly easy to do and requires a substantial investment in tools and training to be accomplished. At MWI, we've been utilizing an in-house apprenticeship program for years and it has continually evolved to serve our in-house needs, but the underlying problem nationwide doesn't seem to be improving as quickly as it should. I worry that the long-term result will be a more throw-away philosophy of vehicle manufacture and ownership, leading to higher costs to repair the vehicles. Neither of these two conditions seems particularly appealing.

 I am fortunate to work with some of the smartest minds in the country as part of my networking. Just breaking ground recently is the *American Skilled Labor Association* (*www. skilledlaborus.com*). I personally know Mike Davidson, the President of this organization and support their commitment to finding ways to help younger people enter this technical field. We believe the answer is to provide educational opportunities for younger students, even

down to middle-school age. They need to be exposed to these intricate and remarkable machines; these *computers on wheels*, and to have a chance to discover an innate excitement for learning about and working with them. Many young people have never held a wrench, turned a screw, and so on. Many have only pushed buttons on their gaming consoles. There is something to be said for learning to be handy and being self-sufficient in the world of machines, even simple ones.

While there will always be a need for the *mechanic*, and now *technician*, it is amazing to think what the auto service industry will be like in 10-20 more years and what kind of work we will actually be doing on the cars.

What will cars look like?

Whether I am there to see it or not, it is my hope that all of the stakeholders, meaning the clients, vendors, and staff never lose the core philosophies that I outline in this book and have instilled into the culture of Motor Works, Inc.

Learning Zone

Do you speak "Car"? Well, you can think of this section as sort of a phrasebook.

So, pay attention. Your car is telling you something!

These days, when you slide in behind the wheel and turn the key or press the "on" button, an introductory bulb check presents the driver with a whole light-and-sound experience. For some people, the various lights and sounds can be confusing. Let's simplify.

First, notice the color of the various lights. They correspond with traffic signals.

RED means STOP

This generally means that some system is alerting the driver about a problem that could be dangerous either to personal safety or to one or more of the car's vital components.

If a red light comes on while you're driving, you really should stop and investigate the problem before proceeding.

YELLOW means CAUTION

If the light that comes on is yellow (or "amber," as the traffic engineers call it), it means caution. There is something the driver may need to do soon to properly care for the car. You should contact your repair shop as soon as you can. It generally doesn't mean that you cannot continue driving, although there are a few exceptions. *See CEL/MIL.*

GREEN **OR BLUE means A-OK**

The other lights that are green or blue generally are reserved for normal functions. Some might include: ECON setting, turn signals, cruise control, etc. Blue also is standard to warn that your bright headlamps are on.

Readers, maybe, just maybe, you might be tempted to disregard an illuminated warning light. Okay, if or when that happens, *right* before you decide to ignore it...*DON'T.*

Just like the story of *The Boy Who Cried Wolf,* when you train yourself to ignore a warning light, you are setting yourself up to miss another important warning from the car in the future. Deal with it today, before it becomes a loan payment, an insurance claim, or worse, tomorrow.

What Are These Warnings For?

Most of the time, the lights and symbols on the dash are easy to understand. Most manufacturers make an effort to standardize the symbols. Let's explain some of them.

ABS = Antilock Brake System

This braking system, originally developed for the aviation industry, made its way over to the automotive world starting in the 1980's.

The premise is simple: a mechanism or sensor compares the rotating speeds of all four wheels and when the difference between any two of them is beyond a certain percentage (meaning a wheel is sliding), the brake pressure you generate by stomping on the brake pedal is *modulated*. It's sort of like pumping the brakes—but really, *really* fast. A sliding tire cannot stop or steer well. But by applying massive braking force while avoiding lockup of the wheel, which is called 'threshold braking,' collision avoidance and control are increased dramatically.

If this light comes on while you are driving, the ABS computer has detected a failure and has put the system into fail-safe mode. This means the brakes will work perfectly normally EXCEPT during a panic stop. You should have the vehicle tested and repaired as soon as possible.

Remember, the system only operates when a wheel is sliding on ice, dirt, water, marbles, etc. You really don't need this system…until you do. So, again: Just before you ignore this warning light…DON'T!

Charging System or Battery Light

 This light will illuminate during startup and then should go out when the engine is running. When this light comes on while you are driving, it means that the vehicle's charging system is malfunctioning and the vehicle is currently running only on the energy stored in the battery.

When this happens, you shouldn't be driving the car. It is possible that the belt that drives the Alternator has failed. This may cause other system problems too. If the particular model car you drive uses that belt to also turn the water pump, for example, continuing the engine use could cause serious engine overheating within only a few minutes.

If the belt is there and still turns the alternator, you could continue for a short distance. Ensure that you have turned off all of the electrical items you can as they will draw the battery down more quickly. The biggest electrical suckers are the A/C or heater blower fan, the wipers, the lights and headlights, the rear window defrost systems or heated seats.

If you are driving and the battery voltage falls too low, the engine will stop and you will be stranded. *I hope the cellphone is charged.*

CEL = Check Engine Light (also known as MIL = Malfunction Indicator Light)

The Check Engine Light has been around for quite a while. With the emission control regulations introduced in the 1970's, more emphasis was put on cleaning up the air, especially by reducing vehicle exhaust gases.

Some of you may not remember carburetors or ignition points and condensers. These old-school parts have become extinct on today's cars primarily because they could not provide tight enough control of the combustion process going on inside the engine.

With the development of faster and better computer chips (yes, Silicone Valley played a huge part), the manufacturers now had *computers* commanding the electronics to inject just the right amount of fuel into the engine at the right time to get closer and closer to λ (lambda).[1]

Because the onboard electronic and computerized systems were becoming so complicated that nobody could efficiently diagnose problems, the automakers (with some prodding from government) got together and decided on a common diagnostic language so the different makes could all communicate with all

---

1   GEEK alert! – In this context, λ roughly represents the ideal gasoline/air mix for combustion, such that all of the oxygen molecules and all of the hydrocarbons are expended, allowing the cleanest gases to exit. It's all in the Stoichiometry. Yep, we're quasi chemists too. Go ahead…Google it.

the technicians. The first systems, called OBD (on-board diagnostics), were rudimentary. The data stored in OBD were so limited that a second version—a "sequel" called OBD II—was created. This second-generation system enabled the on-board testing programs to transmit a significant data stream that was much more helpful in tracking down odd problems.

Carburetors and ignition points were MECHANICAL objects and MECHANICS could fix them. The modern systems are TECHNOLOGICALLY advanced and so we need TECHNICIANS to be able to fix them. That's how your car guy's job title got changed. And it's not just a matter of changing the terminology in an attempt to sound more impressive: it reflects a whole new category of job requirements. There are multiple computers in modern cars that require a whole different level of knowledge to service. The tools are different, the skill sets are different, and the training is different. Time marches on. Automotive information systems continue to improve to keep pace with the explosion of computer functions. These days, repair shops must invest in computer interfaces and related equipment, special tools, and training. If your repair shop doesn't stay current on these developments, it will be unable to professionally service your car in the near future. Your car's main engine management computer continuously monitors more than 75 parameters to keep every system running smoothly and efficiently as you drive along. Some of the monitors are routine, like making sure that you tightened the gas cap enough to prevent fuel vapors (and your money) from escaping into the atmosphere. Some tests are performed after a precise number of drive cycles or under very specific driving conditions.

Other functions monitor systems that are more important to the safety of the vehicle's emission equipment and are in continuous test mode. For example, one test compares signals from two exhaust sensors, allowing the main computer to monitor the efficiency of the catalytic converter. The converter is responsible for changing the chemical composition of the exhaust before it leaves the vehicle. Any malfunction that could cause damage to this rather expensive part will enter a "trouble" code in the computer's memory, and turn the Check Engine light on in flash mode. If this light comes on and flashes continuously, you should slow and curtail driving and have your car professionally tested as soon as possible.

Less worrisome is when the (usually YELLOW) light comes on and stays on. The computer has detected a failure in one of the many systems of the car, set a trouble code in its memory and illuminated the warning light. The car is perfectly drivable for the time being. Try to take note of the specific conditions that were present when the light appeared. This yellow light means you need to pay a visit to your shop for testing as soon as is convenient.

SRS = Supplementary Restraint System

The SRS is commonly known as the air-bag system. The key word here is supplementary. That means it is a supplement to your seat belts and shoulder harnesses. *You should ALWAYS wear your seatbelt.*

If the airbag or SRS light (usually RED) comes on while driving, the SRS control computer has detected a problem in the one of the components and has gone into fail-safe mode. The airbags will not deploy if an accident occurs. Airbags only deploy in certain types of collisions in which the g-force is severe enough to cause injury to the occupants. The entire deployment process occurs violently and is over before you can even realize it has happened. It really IS that fast.

The SRS and seatbelt systems are designed to do everything possible to lessen injury or even save your life. Problems with the systems are not all that common. Parts can be rather expensive.

Smart Air Bag Light:

This system is part of the SRS system. These days, almost all cars are equipped with smart air bags. Sensors in the front passenger seat measure the weight and positioning of the occupant.

Depending on the weight of the person or object in that seat, the air bag may deploy with lower force or may not deploy at all. If there is a small child in the front seat, the sensor detects it. If the weight in the front seat does not meet a minimum established by the manufacturer, the smart air bag light will come on to let you know that the airbag is off on the passenger side and will not deploy in the event of a collision. This light is usually YELLOW.

Not a bubble gum blowing light

The reason the airbag doesn't deploy with a child in the front passenger seat is because research and controlled testing have determined that small children may not withstand the violent deployment of an airbag without severe injury or death.

The inside of an airbag contains a substance that burns super-fast and causes expanding gases to inflate the bags. When triggered, the bag inflation occurs so fast that a human cannot detect deployment until it is over and the bag has deflated. Super-slow motion videography reveals that the bag reaches the occupant's face almost instantaneously and then slows the body's forward progression at a more controlled speed. Sometimes, a heavy object or objects on the front passenger seat might trigger the air bag to turn off. Also, if a passenger isn't sitting upright in the seat or is leaning on the door, the warning may illuminate.

TCS = Traction Control System

No, these aren't snakes following your car

To keep the car from losing traction and possibly causing an accident, many cars come with a TCS. Onboard computers monitor wheel speeds and braking pressures to determine if one or more wheels lose traction; if that happens, they automatically transfer power to the wheels that are still grabbing the pavement. The TCS also has some control over the engine output to keep an overactive right foot from inadvertently causing loss of control. Both two-wheel drive and all-wheel drive (AWD) vehicles utilize these systems.

Some AWD vehicles also have a special mode that locks all four wheels together. This mode is only used at extremely low speeds and is designed to aid in extricating the vehicle from snow, ice, mud, sand, etc.

During the starting procedure, the TCS light comes on momentarily as the system activates a self-test. If there's a failure in the system, the light (which is usually YELLOW) will stay on. The car can still be driven, although the traction control will not be available. That is when you need to take your vehicle in for testing. On some models, the TCS light will illuminate when the system is actually adjusting the car to prevent slip. This would be a normal driver notification to be careful.

Temperature Light:

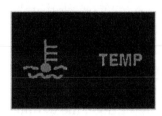

In recent model years, this light has replaced the old engine-temperature gauge on many cars. When you first start the car, and see a blue "C" with a thermometer icon, this means the engine isn't warmed up yet. It is okay to drive with this light on (gently, please). The "Uh-Oh"

temperature light will always be red, indicating that you need to shut the car down as soon as possible. No kidding; it is in your best interest to stop driving immediately to investigate the problem. Many times, at MWI we have seen vehicles that are overheated so badly, their engines require major repairs that cost thousands of dollars. If a problem is caught early, much of your hard-earned money can usually be saved.

When the RED temperature light comes on, you should pull over as quickly as you safely can, then turn the engine off.

After that, the first step in the troubleshooting process is to make sure that your coolant level is full. But be careful! You have to use extreme caution when removing the radiator cap. When a car is still hot, the radiator's contents are under pressure, and you can be burned by the scalding hot steam and coolant when you release the cap. It is best to let the car sit for several hours to cool down before adding coolant.

The best way to handle this problem is to subscribe to preventive maintenance instead of waiting for an event to occur. Have your professional technician inspect the cooling system on a regular basis.

Oil Warning Light:

This is one of the most important warnings the car can give you. For this section, I'd like you to think of the oil warning light as a blood pressure warning light. The oil in the engine is like the blood in your body. Not enough blood or blood pressure can make for a really bad day.

If the engine loses oil pressure, the oil light is going to come on. That light will be RED because you need to shut the engine down quickly. If the oil pressure is too low, internal damage

to the engine is imminent. The damage would be similar to driving without any oil in the engine at all. This is where it gets very costly, very quickly.

To clarify, you can be low on oil level and still have oil pressure. The oil light may not let you know that you are low on oil until you're out of oil altogether.

In other words: Even when you're a quart or two low on oil, there's still enough oil in the engine to produce enough oil pressure to keep the oil light from turning on. But the lower your oil level, the more stress and damage to your engine is possible. Potentially, you could have a dangerously low oil level in the engine and no indicator light to warn you. That's why regular oil changes are so important, and so is checking the oil level often.

Dashboard Gauges

In addition to dashboard lights, many cars have dashboard gauges. The following are the primary gauges you'll find on the dashboard of vehicles today. They provide a quick and easy way to tell how well the car is functioning.

Temperature Gauge:

Typically, you will find this gauge in the instrument cluster by looking for the universal symbol of a thermometer in liquid. This gauge monitors the temperature of the coolant that circulates through the engine and heating system.

As you probably could guess, blue or "C" stands for cold and red or "H" stands for hot. On most gauges, normal operating temperature is indicated when the needle is about midway up the gauge. If the gauge reads too cool or too hot, bad things can happen.

If the thermostat fails, for example, the engine might take a very long time to reach normal operating temperature. That wastes fuel and reduces overall vehicle efficiency as well as heater output.

Alternatively, engine overheating will almost always damage today's engines and can get very costly alarmingly fast.

Get used to what your car's "normal" looks like and report any readings that deviate from that to your technician.

Tachometer:

The tachometer indicates how many times the engine crankshaft rotates, displaying engine speed in *revolutions per minute* or *"RPM"*. When at idle, most tachometers read at or below "1" which means one thousand revolutions per minute.

Once the engine reaches normal operating temperature, you will see the gauge point to about two-thirds of the way from "0" to "1," or around the 650-750 RPM range at idle. If you drive a hybrid that features an engine-stop function, this gauge will drop to zero at stoplights; an accompanying light usually appears on the dash. That's a normal situation.

It can be helpful to keep an eye on the tachometer. The RPM should drop each time the transmission shifts into a higher gear, increasing fuel economy. If you notice that the engine appears to be running at higher RPM than normal, it may indicate that something is not right—that the engine is working harder than usual.

Voltage Gauge:

This gauge shows the relative condition of the car's electrical system. Most cars today run on standard 12-volt electrical systems. Under normal operating conditions, the gauge should read around 14 volts.

When you turn the ignition key, the gauge indicates the voltage level in the battery. Once the engine is running, it reads the voltage in the charging system that runs the car's overall electrical system.

The two main components of the charging system include the B*attery* and the *Alternator.* The Alternator is responsible for generating electricity to operate all of the vehicle systems while the engine is running; the battery is basically a storage device that provides the electricity needed to start the car.

If the voltage gauge reads consistently low or high, the electrical system needs to be tested. The gauge might be warning you of an impending breakdown because of a potential electrical component failure.

A hybrid vehicle includes additional systems that operate the electrical components for driving and energy reclamation conditions. Those energy gauges provide a graphic representation of the energy available for use in the hybrid battery.

Fuel Gauge:

While "E" means *excellence* in some contexts, in this case it means you're getting ready to walk home – Empty. Note the little arrow next to the icon of a gas pump: it indicates which side of the vehicle the gas filler is on.

In modern cars, the electric fuel pump that supplies gas to the engine is located *inside* the fuel tank. Having enough fuel in the tank keeps that pump cool, which helps extend its life. Running completely out of fuel will, in certain situations, cause the main fuel pump to fail, requiring a much more costly repair (also resulting in a really ticked-off significant other…don't ask how I know…I just do).

As a general rule, you should keep a minimum of a quarter tank of fuel in your car at all times—even more in the winter, during which weather conditions could allow moisture to condense inside the tank. This doesn't happen very much on modern cars, but it still IS possible.

Pay attention if your car has a low-fuel warning light as well. This light might just be a yellow circle on the fuel gauge or it might look like a gas pump. It will come on when the tank gets down to its last 1 or 2 gallons. Do yourself a favor and refuel at the earliest opportunity.

Also, if you happen to be touring parts of the country that may not have gas stations for miles and miles, fuel refills will become even more necessary when the opportunities arise. Let's just say, I've run out on the Chesapeake Bay Bridge, another time when we were going to my Sister-In-Law's wedding. I have run dangerously low while driving out west, miles from a station on a couple of occasions. My advice–*don't be a fool...just refuel.*

Last thing; if you pull into a gas station and see that the giant tanker truck is there refilling their underground tanks, go to another gas station if you can. The refilling process can churn up dirt and debris if their tanks are older. Sometimes the station managers don't service the gas pump filters as they should. This habit could save you a big problem with clogged fuel injectors or other fuel system trouble if dirt and debris is pumped into your tank.

Speedometer – Odometer – Trip odometers:

I figure that you pretty much know that the SPEEDOMETER is displaying the speed of the vehicle, displayed in miles per hour (unless you're in another country that reads in the metric KPH or *kilometers per hour*).

The ODOMETER tracks the cumulative mileage on your vehicle. The TRIP ODOMETER is a temporary mileage tracker that can be reset during fuel stops or—well, anytime you want, really. Some models include more than one trip odometer so that the driver can track and calculate fuel mileage at fill ups while simultaneously tracking the total mileage of the trip.

The accuracy of the speedometers and odometers has improved over the years. Today's cars have digital odometers that cannot be tampered with, protecting the value and integrity when a car is resold. No more "rolling back" the mileage. Bad guys are still out there, but this is one trick that's been removed from their bag.

When buying tires, it's very important that the new tires are the same size as the original tires. Changes here will affect the accuracy of the speedometer and odometer. This can cause more problems in other systems as well.

Technical Tidbits

What is a Timing Belt?

Four-cycle internal combustion engines use a *camshaft* to open and close the intake and exhaust valves. This shaft has an egg-shaped CAM for each valve that pushes open the intake and exhaust valves in the proper sequence.

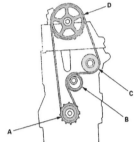

-1 Drive pulley (A).
-2 Tensioner pulley (B).
-3 Water pump pulley (C).
-4 Camshaft pulley (D).

The camshaft is *timed or synchronized* with the crankshaft (what the pistons are attached to). In completing the four cycles there are two revolutions of the crankshaft for every revolution of the camshaft. No matter how fast or slow the engine goes, this ratio stays the same. The timing belt governs that ratio. It has rounded "teeth" that engage with sprockets on both the crankshaft and the camshaft.

Replacing the timing belt is not especially difficult although there is usually quite a bit of disassembly to gain access to it. MWI suggests replacing the outer drive belts and water pump at the same time as the timing belt because water pumps are driven by the timing belt and the outer belts must be removed anyway. It is in the car owner's best interest to replace these items together as it represents the best use of your repair dollar. Since this function is critical to the life and operation of the engine, we strongly recommend using only original parts.

Fogged Glass

If you've ever seen somebody driving a vehicle with the insides of all the windows completely fogged, it was a memorable experience, wasn't it? How do you avoid being that driver? Remember to set your Fresh/ Recirculate button to "fresh," so outside air is brought in. Otherwise, the moisture in our clothing and our breath condenses on the inside of the cool glass, sometimes quickly enough to cause the windows to fog. Heavy breathing can do that too, so pull over before engaging in heavy breathing. Better yet, get a room. Many cars these days automatically engage the A/C system when set to defrost. This dehumidifies the air and evaporates the fog quickly.

Remember to use the A/C for at least 10 minutes each month, including the cold months. This helps keep the A/C system seals in good condition.

What is a Catalytic Converter?

In the exhaust system, the hot gases pass through a substrate: a ceramic honeycomb that is embedded with the precious-metal elements platinum, palladium, rhodium and cerium. These elements act as catalysts that cause a chemical conversion in the makeup of the gasses. The result is a cleaner emission and a cleaner environment.

Engine misfires can cause the catalytic substrate to overheat. The substrate can melt or break into pieces. Because these precious-metal elements are rare, catalytic converters are inherently expensive; so, if your car isn't running right or you notice a flashing check-engine light, have the car checked right away before you ruin your converter.

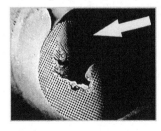

This image was taken looking down into the **catalytic converter,** which is located in the exhaust system. There is a big part of the substrate missing.

At MWI, we routinely perform complete emission systems diagnosis and repair! MWI also partners with the Montgomery County (Maryland) Department of Environmental Protection.

Radiator Hose Failure

Under the hood will be many hoses. Some carry engine coolant between the engine and the radiator. The coolant is what is responsible for keeping the engine from overheating.

Pictured here is an upper radiator hose from an Acura that is about to pop. This was a first-time client—and boy, were we surprised when we opened the hood.

Most under-hood hoses last a long, long time, but they should be scrutinized or replaced after 10 years to prevent a leak and/or overheating incident. Remember, overheating one of these engines can drastically shorten its life.

Motor Works regularly evaluates cooling system component conditions during routine maintenance. Ask your service provider to do the same.

What is a "CV Boot"?

On front-wheel-drive and all-wheel-drive cars, *axle shafts* connect the transmission with the wheels, driving the vehicle along. The axles must flex, allowing the suspension to move up and down and the front wheels to turn right and left, while at the same time transmitting the driving force from the engine to the wheels.

The part that simultaneously enables the axle flex while transmitting the driving force is called a drive axle joint, and is also known as a *constant velocity* (or CV) joint. The CV Boot is a ribbed, rubber flexible boot that keeps water and dirt out of the joint and the special grease inside the joint. Pictured above is a view of a front, outer CV boot that has torn open.

The greasy mass inside is the actual joint itself. If the car is driven in this condition, the exposed grease is quickly slung out by centrifugal force as the axle rotates, and the joint subsequently becomes contaminated with sand, dirt, rocks, and water, rapidly wearing the joint components. Excessive wear may necessitate replacement of the entire axle shaft assembly, a much more expensive proposition than replacing the boot itself.

The Vehicle Owner – Your Part

Why Preventive Maintenance?

You can think of preventive maintenance (P/M) as an investment, or even as something like setting aside some savings. You will realize a return on the P/M "investment". P/M gives you:

Here's the goal

- ➲ Peace of Mind–It's hard to put a price on your peace of mind – lower stress – less worry.

- ➲ No Surprises – Servicing is done on YOUR terms and on your schedule.

- ➲ Safety & Convenience – P/M catches little problems before they become huge, and possibly life-threatening, incidents. Compared with the national average. MWI clients are, on average, 248% LESS LIKELY to be towed with a breakdown. It's true!

- ➲ Cost–This might seem counterintuitive. Many people might think they're saving money by avoiding a visit to the repair shop for P/M when "nothing is wrong." The opposite is true. P/M retains the vehicle's highest resale value. A complete service history is valuable when selling your current car.

This is important: *The least expensive vehicle to own is the one you're driving right now.* Of course, there are exceptions to every rule; but in a wide majority of cases, maintaining your vehicle so that you can keep it for a long time is the most economical approach—by far—to the major investment that owning an auto represents.

What You Should Focus On

Pay attention to your car and the way you interact with it. Even though it is a machine, respect the mechanisms and the way it becomes an extension of your body when you drive.

Notice things. No one knows your car like you do, and when you pay attention to how it feels, sounds, smells, handles, and operates, you'll be in the best position to identify when something has changed—when something doesn't work or act the same. These can be the early warning signs that might help avoid a costly repair later on.

Remember incidents. Big pot holes, driving headlong into those puddles that seem more like mini-lakes, having to jam on the brakes to avoid a deer: these are also things that could be the root of problems not yet discovered.

Communicate. Your service provider should be asking you questions—sometimes rather strange ones, depending on your perceived concern. Examples might be: Was it the first start of the day? Was it raining? How fast were you going? What day did you first notice this? Were you in a parking garage when you heard it? How long has this been going on? Are you the only driver? Do you have any young/new drivers in the house? These types of questions begin to guide the shop towards a more efficient set of tests to determine the exact cause of the condition you are describing.

Knowledge is power. You NEED to know what's going on

with your car so you can proactively make informed decisions that are in your own best interest. At MWI, we sometimes run into people who just don't want to know what is going on with their car, and we think that this hide-your-head philosophy is not at all useful. The problems don't cease to exist just because you choose not to look at them. They will eventually jump up and bite you, usually when you least expect it.

Don't procrastinate. Seriously, it gets exponentially more expensive to wait in most situations.

Engine Damage – What We're Trying to Avoid

 In this picture, the little red finger is pointing to the area of this exhaust valve that has burned away.

Since the engine is basically a pump, the engine valves keep the gasses flowing in the proper direction from the air filter all the way to the exhaust tailpipe.

A burned valve prevents the cylinder from properly producing power and causes a serious emissions problem.

Regular valve clearance adjustments, usually performed during routine annual maintenance services, would have prevented this very costly repair.

Tire Wear – Extreme

Please note the angle with which the tire tread is worn towards the insides. These came off the rear axle of a Civic that hit something hard enough to bend a rear control arm and radically change the rear wheel alignment. The tires were ruined in a very short time. The inner part of the tread scrubbed the pavement because the tires were steering away from each other.

At MWI, we routinely monitor the tire condition by checking the tread wear and pressures during every visit. Your techs should too.

Things That You Can Do (or Learn) to Help Your Car

In the old days, if a car had its hood open and it began to rain, some (if not many) of the raindrops could fall straight through to the pavement without touching any part of the engine. That doesn't happen with newer cars—there's lot more stuff under the hood these days, and it's a lot more complicated. Here are a few tips to help you with checking things out under the hood. Remember though, some things can be a little more dangerous in there, especially on Hybrid vehicles. Use common sense and caution, okay?

Open the hood

Usually on the left kick panel, to the left of the driver's left foot, you should find a release lever with an image of a car with its hood up. With a finger, pull it out and away from the panel and you should hear a "clunk" as the latch

releases. The lever is spring-loaded, so it should pop back to its normal position by itself.

Walk around to the front of the car. Reach one hand between the bottom of the hood and the grille to find the secondary release lever. This safety system prevents the hood from flying open while the car is motion and blocking the driver's view if the primary latch should fail or otherwise

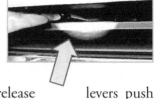

be left unlocked. Most secondary release levers push UP to release, thereby allowing the hood to open.

Note: On some cars, the secondary latch needs to move left or right to release.) After popping the secondary release, you can lift the hood.

Hood prop-rod clip

Some hoods have automatic, gas-filled supports that will take the weight of the hood and hold it completely open. Other cars use a prop-rod. If yours does too, snap the rod loose from its clip by pulling up on it, then raise it up to meet the hood. Look for an embossed arrow and a special hole in the underside of the hood where the end of the prop-rod will fit properly to support the hood. USE IT! You don't want the type of a headache that accompanies the hood banging down on your head.

What's under the hood?

There is likely a diagram in your owner's manual that looks kind of like this. *This one is courtesy of my wife's 2013 Honda CR-V's owner's manual.*

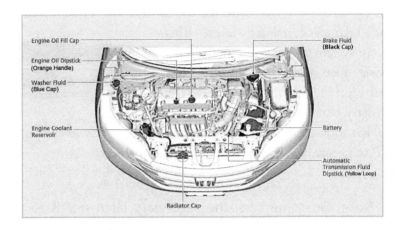

When you look around under your own car's hood, pay attention to the various colors of things you'll find there. Most cars use colors to help identify different service components.

Orange	Engine oil dipstick
Yellow	Transmission oil dipstick
Blue	Windshield washer fluid
Black	Brake fluid

I took the following pictures of my car. Can you identify some of these items on your own car?

Prop-rod clip, transmission dipstick, brake fluid reservoir and the battery

Oil dipstick

How to check the engine oil

1. Park the vehicle on level ground

2. Wait 3 minutes or so after shutting the engine off so the oil can return to the sump.

3. Remove the oil dipstick

4. Wipe the oil off the dipstick with a rag or paper towel

5. Reinsert the dipstick all the way in

6. Remove it again and check the oil level. It should be between the upper and lower holes (or marks) at the end of the dipstick.

7. Add oil only if necessary. Refer to the oil cap and/or your owner's manual for the proper type of oil for your car.

8. When you do have to add oil, note the amount you added and the vehicle's mileage. Usually, a well-maintained car will not need to have oil added between maintenance stops. However, running an engine that is low on oil is asking for big trouble.

9. Do not overfill the engine with oil. This too can cause engine damage.

How to check the engine coolant level

1. Locate the coolant overflow bottle. It is usually mounted close to the radiator. If you see a small black hose just to the side of the radiator cap, follow it to the tank.

2. The level of fluid in the tank should be visible through the tank itself.

3. The level should be between the MIN and MAX lines embossed on the tank.

4. If the tank is low, add the proper engine coolant- consult your owner's manual for details.

If the tank is OUT altogether, wait until the engine is cool before removing the radiator cap (1/4 turn counterclockwise) and check its level as well. Advise your service provider if you have to add a significant amount of coolant, as it is not supposed to be consumed by the engine or leak from any engine component.

NOTE: DO NOT OPEN THE RADIATOR PRESSURE CAP WHEN THE ENGINE IS HOT – PERSONAL INJURY AND BURNS COULD RESULT!

How to check the automatic transmission oil level

1. This should be done with the engine turned off after having reached normal operating temperature.

2. Park on level ground.

3. Remove the transmission dipstick (usually a yellow loop or handle).

4. Wipe it with a paper towel or rag. Reinsert it all the way in.

5. Remove the dipstick again and check the fluid level. It should be between the upper and lower marks in the HOT range.

6. If you need to add fluid, check your owner's manual for the proper type for your car.

7. Fluid is usually added in small quantities through the dipstick tube. It's best to use a funnel.

8. You should not have to add transmission fluid between service stops. If you need to add some, it would be wise to contact your service provider and have the car looked at. It should not be using or leaking fluid.

How to check the Brake fluid level

1. Find the translucent white reservoir.

2. The fluid is usually caramel colored and the level should be between the MIN and MAX lines.

3. If the fluid is below the MIN line, you should contact your service provider for a professional evaluation. The car should neither use nor leak brake fluid from anywhere.

4. If you have to add some, use only DOT3 or DOT4 brake fluid (commercially available) from a sealed container. Brake fluid is *hygroscopic* and absorbs moisture from the air. Contaminated brake fluid can damage brake hydraulic system components, which generally makes for a bad day.

Brake fluid reservoir

How to check the windshield washer fluid level

1. Locate the washer fluid reservoir cap (usually blue)

2. Many cars incorporate a type of dipstick as part of or below the blue snap in cap.

3. Pull out and check the fluid level.

4. Add Windshield Washer fluid (commercially available) but do not overfill the tank.

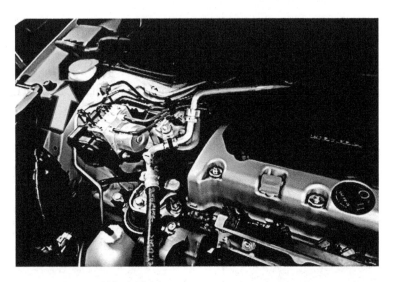

Windshield washer reservoir tank cap

Windshield Haze Tip

Here's a safety tip... Especially in the late autumn and wintertime, the sun's angle can wreak havoc with your ability to see through the haze that builds up on the inside of our windshields.

A single sheet of crumpled-up newsprint is great for buffing the inside of the glass and removing the haze (and it's a great way to recycle!).

The hazy chemical buildup is caused by the off-gassing of the dashboard and interior's vinyl and plastic components–especially when they bake in full sun.

Keep it clean, inside and out

1. Spilled coffee and sodas can really screw up switches and mechanisms around the center console.

2. Wash the car regularly. Use commercially available car wash soap and soft brushes or sponges designed to avoid paint scratches. Car washing is ESPECIALLY important after you've been driving in snow or ice on roads that have been treated with salt or brine. This also means if you live or visit an area where salt water is present…like the beach. Take it to a car wash and get the undercarriage washed. The salt compound tends to eat cars. Yuck!

3. Vacuum the carpets and mats.

4. Have the body waxed at least once each year to protect the paint and finish

How to check the tire pressures and condition

1. This is really important for your safety. Underinflated and overinflated tires wear faster (and in weird patterns), increase fuel consumption, cause the car to handle poorly, and might fail at high speeds from overheating. So… just before you ignore this…DON'T!

2. Every day before you leave, make a habit out of looking at your tires as you walk up to your car. If one appears lower than the others, check it out. Get out your tire gauge. What? You don't have one? Just get one (commercially available) or stop by  your service provider's shop and they'll be happy to check them for you. Also, most gas-station air pumps include built-in gauges.

3. Before taking a family vacation or a long trip, you should check your tire pressures even if they don't look low.

4. Check the tire pressures with the tires cool, before you drive in the morning.

5. Pay attention to any bumps or bulges on the sidewall of the tires or screws and nails in the treads. Some of us have more challenges parking near curbs than others. If there are any cuts in the tire, have them looked at by a professional immediately. The last thing anyone wants is for you to have a blowout on the highway.

6. Most cars have a label some-where on the driver-side door jamb that will give the suggested cold tire pressures for your car. It is my opinion  that you can safely increase the tire pressures by 4 pounds per square inch (PSI) to avoid TPMS false alarms of the "seasonal-loss" variety.

7. If you do see a TPMS warn-ing light, stop immediately and investigate. If none of the tires are flat, you can drive conservatively to your service provider and have the problem investigated.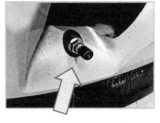

8. Make sure that there is a valve cap on your tire valve stems, especially if your car has a TPMS system. If it does, use only plastic (special sized) valve caps. Many TPMS sensors are pricey and metal valve caps can destroy them.

How to Find a Competent Repair Shop

If you're moving out of your current area, one of the best steps you can take to find a reliable new repair shop is to ask your current one. Most shops are in some kind of network or association, so your current shop's proprietor may know a good shop in the area where you are relocating.

If you're looking for a reliable repair shop in your current locale, here are some tips about finding one you will be happy with. Do some investigation.

1. Ask friends and coworkers who they use and are satisfied with.

2. Do an online search for your particular area or make and model of vehicle you own such as *Honda repairs Rockville Maryland.*

3. Spend some time on a shop's website. Is it easy to navigate? Is it informative? Does the shop's personality shine through?

4. Read some of their testimonials and online reviews. *Angie's List, Google, Yahoo Yelp,* and your local *Better Business Bureau* are some of the more popular places to find them. Be careful with these—online reviews can be manipulated by unscrupulous businesses *or* reviewers. Use common sense.

5. Check with your local Office of Consumer Protection to determine their rating or if there are many un-settled claims.

Once you've narrowed your choices to a short list, call one of the shops and schedule a visit or have them perform a small job such as an oil-and-lube service. Try to arrange to have this done while you wait.

When you arrive, pay attention to how you are treated and how proficient they seem. Are they pleasant and business-like? Is the waiting area clean? Are the necessary certifications displayed prominently?

Take note of how the employees interact with each other and with the other customers. Notice how they answer the phone. If possible, watch the way they handle your car.

Find out if their technicians are fully certified and if they participate in continuing education and training programs.

Are they technologically savvy? Do they use a computer system to maintain proper recordkeeping? Do they have the necessary tools and equipment to communicate with your car's onboard computer?

Ask them if they utilize any system of reminders to let you know when it's time for service. Do they have a schedule in place to keep your car well maintained?

An oil, lube, and filter service should take about 20 minutes to complete. During that time, you should be able to start to determine if this shop is a good fit for you. Trust your gut.

How to Work with Your Repair Shop

As I have stated in other areas of this book, having a great relationship with your repair shop requires a few things.

First of all, the relationship must be based on mutual respect. This means that you benefit from a deeper understanding and respect for the individuals at the shop, and they understand your needs and respect you as their client. Work together with the shop as a partnership, understanding that the relationship is not adversarial, but rather collaborative.

Second, clearly communicate needs. Explain exactly what's

going on with the car, your individual concerns, including other stresses in your life such as your schedule, transportation needs, or budget constraints. A competent Service Advisor will be listening intently, asking pertinent questions and taking

Greg with Ms. Smith, another long-term client

notes in order to help identify and avoid possible problems during your visit.

Third, planning is paramount. Look ahead to project and anticipate possible stress points. This allows all of the stakeholders in the relationship to "act upon" rather than "react to." Essentially, it's much more efficient, smooth and comfortable when you know what's going to happen.

Noises – Do you hear what I hear?

One of the greatest things about car ownership is really getting to know your car. You have five senses—hearing, sight, smell, taste, and touch. You can use your senses (well—with the exception of taste) to know what is normal for *your* car so you'll recognize when something has changed.

When it comes to hearing noises that you know are *not normal—not what you are used to hearing*—one of the best things you can do is to know how to "show the noise."

Being able to "show the noise" is much more helpful to your technician than your earnest efforts to explain the noise. The first step is to pay attention to your car, and to take note of when you first heard the noise.

Ask yourself: What were the conditions when I heard the

noise? Was I on the highway, or at a stoplight? Was I backing out of a driveway? Was it cold out? Was it raining? If you can be descriptive here, you're saving yourself money and time by  helping the technician zero in on the cause quickly.

Experienced technicians can typically recognize many noises that you may not identify as a problem. It's not at all like the television ads in which customers make embarrassing noises and a "tech" says, "oh, it's just your idle…no big deal" …or something equally inaccurate.

Even so, some common types of noise can be described in written form.

- ⟳ Scraping (high-pitched), like a metal rake on a sidewalk

- ⟳ Scraping (low-pitched), like something rubbing or grinding on a metal plate.

- ⟳ Squeaks (high-pitched and irregular), like two items rubbing together.

- ⟳ Squeaks (high-pitched and consistent) when something is applied, like stepping on the brakes

- ⟳ Squeals (intermittent), like tires squealing on pavement, or perhaps like a slipping belt

- ⟳ Clunk (heavy), over bumps, felt through steering, seat or floor.

- ⟳ Clicks or Pops – could be intermittent – rapid? With speed

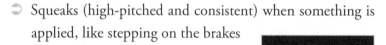

of wheels? When accelerating and turning? Only when braking heavily?

- Crunching or Groaning – usually over speed humps – worse in cold weather

- Moaning – when going fast? Wind noise? Only when the A/C is on?

- Rattle – low or heavy – something's loose – over bumps

- Rattle – high – like gravel in a metal pan

At MWI, things that we commonly see as the causes for unusual noises include:

- Audible sensors for the brake pad wear (doing what they are supposed to)

- Rocks embedded in the front brake caliper scraping on the rotating brake disc (no big deal)

- Internal engine component problems (uh-oh)

- Loose dashboard components or windows not aligned

- Glass bits still inside the door (after window replacement)

- Poor quality brake components (or the aftermath of a poorly done installation)

- Low tire pressures

- Worn or loose drive belts

- Worn suspension, sway bar links or rubber bushings, steering components, or failed wheel bearings (whirring)

- Windshield seal or window leaks, or problems with a/c control valves

- Debris in the cabin air blower fan

- Too much junk in the trunk (golf clubs are noisy), or loose spare-tire mounts

- Rusted and/or cracked exhaust component heat shields

This is (of course) a partial list, provided mostly to inform motorists about matters they are usually curious about at one time or another. It is not intended as a definitive guide to self-diagnosis! If you are hearing something that sounds unusual to you, don't hesitate to ask your service person.

They may ask you some questions like the ones listed below – try to be prepared to answer. If they don't ask, volunteer the information.

The list includes several questions discussed earlier. Here are a few:

- Was it cold outside when you first heard the noise?

- Was it raining?

- Were you sitting still (at a stoplight)?

- Were you driving at highway speeds?

- How long has it been doing this (when did you first notice)?

- Have there been any memorable "incidents" lately?

- Is there a new driver in the home?

- Were any mechanical or body repairs done recently?

- Can you recount the driving conditions just before you noticed the noise?

> **Tip:** If you're in doubt, pull out your smartphone and make a brief audio or video recording. Be sure to do this safely (if at speed, have a passenger do this for you)! Mail it as an attachment to info@motor-works.com and we'll do our best to identify it for proper testing. This might end up saving you expense as well.

Emergencies – How NOT to Freak Out

I love sayings. One of my favorites goes like this: *The best way to avoid an accident is to NOT be present at the point of impact.*

Putting the smart-aleck humor aside, there's actually good advice in that saying. The likelihood of a roadside emergency can and absolutely should be reduced by anticipating the possibilities and taking steps to mitigate the risks that these possibilities will ever occur.

This being said, we cannot eliminate risk altogether. Stuff happens. Machines break. Drivers screw up.

Make sure to have a cell phone that works and some friends or family on the other end of the phone who can help when needed. Your service provider should be there for you too; I know we are. Call us at 301-424-2800 and if we can't answer, leave a voice mail message. Our state-of-the-art communications technology alerts us when a message comes in. Don't be afraid to ask for help. Auto clubs, some insurance policies, and some auto makers also offer roadside assistance plans.

How to Change a Flat Tire

If you've never changed a flat before, let me encourage you to practice doing so in the safety of your garage or driveway. Become familiar with the tools and the procedure. Follow the directions given in the owner's manual. If you have children of or near driving age, demonstrate the technique to them and then let them duplicate the process. The last thing you want to do is begin to learn how to change a flat when you're pulled off on the side of a road!

Newer vehicles have a tire pressure monitoring system (TPMS) that will indicate when you have a low tire. If that light comes on, you need to quickly find a safe place to pull over so you can investigate the situation and, possibly, change the tire.

Tires can go flat over a short *or* a long period of time, depending on the size of the leak. When you need to change a tire, *the most dangerous place for you to change it is on the shoulder of an interstate (or similar) highway.* If possible, get off the highway, even if that means driving on the shoulder at a very slow speed with your flashers on until you can exit—or at least to an area of the road where you can safely pull off the road (which to me is at least 20 feet from the edge of the freeway). Ideally, you want to exit and get to a safe location off the freeway, where you can raise the car using the tools provided. A lighted area is preferable if this happens at night. The **owner's manual** will tell you the exact location where you must place the jack underneath the car in order to raise the vehicle safely. You can damage the car, become injured, or both if you place the jack incorrectly. Make certain the emergency brake is on securely.

Most cars are equipped with the wrench (sometimes combined with a tire iron) you use to loosen and tighten the lug nuts. To make it easier to change the tire, position the wrench in such a way that you can use your leg and body weight, if needed, to loosen 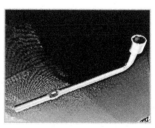 each lug nut. Always loosen (but don't remove) the lug nuts *before* you raise the car high enough that the tire is off the ground. It's much easier to get the nuts loose if you do it that way.

When putting the spare tire on, be sure to start each of the lug nuts by hand. Remember to put the beveled edge of the lug nut toward the wheel. Then, with your tire iron, tighten them in

 an "opposing" or "star" pattern. This means, don't tighten them in adjacent order. Instead, tighten one, then skip the next one, tighten the third one, then skip one and tighten the fifth one, and so on. Eventually, all five nuts will be tight. If your car has four lug nuts, just tighten them in opposite pairs.

Checklist for Changing a Flat Tire

- ✓ Slow the vehicle safely – put the emergency flashers on
- ✓ Stop in a safe, flat location away from speeding traffic
- ✓ Make SURE the emergency brake is ON!
- ✓ Locate the jack, tools and spare tire
- ✓ Position the jack underneath the proper jacking point
- ✓ Raise the vehicle slightly (wheel still on the ground)
- ✓ Loosen all lug nuts ¼ turn on the wheel.
- ✓ Raise the vehicle until the flat tire is off the ground
- ✓ Remove the lug nuts and remove the flat tire & wheel
- ✓ Install the spare tire onto the lug studs
- ✓ Install lug nuts (beveled side toward wheel) & snug
- ✓ Lower the vehicle until the tire is on the ground
- ✓ Tighten each lug nut in an opposing sequence
- ✓ Lower vehicle and remove jack. Stow tools and flat tire
- ✓ Drive at a reduced speed with temporary spare
- ✓ Recheck lug tightness after 20 miles or so

How to Manage a Breakdown

You should be familiar enough with your car and its gauges to know what *normal* is, so when the gauges are not within normal range, you will realize something is wrong.

While driving, if you begin to feel something about the function of your car that you are unsure about, or hear a new noise, cautiously move into the right lane. You do *not* want your vehicle to be disabled in the left lane or in the median of a freeway. Always try to get to a safe location to manage a breakdown—not only for your sake, but for that of your passengers and your car.

If your vehicle begins to overheat, the gauges or lights will indicate it, so keep an eye on them. If your vehicle *is* overheating, turn the engine off as soon as possible.

The second thing you should do during a breakdown is to make a call. These days most people carry cell phones. I recommend you keep numbers for a towing company, motor club or repair shop in your phone for such an emergency.

Make sure you're in a safe spot and keep passengers a safe distance from the highway as you wait for help to arrive. This will decrease your risk of an accident.

Managing a breakdown, though sometimes nerve-wracking and inconvenient, is not that complicated. Try to remember the following:

Don't panic, think safety and call for assistance.

How to jump start a car

Jump (or *boost*) starting a car essentially uses electricity from the good battery to supplement the bad one.

How exactly do you jump a car with a dead battery? Be sure to maneuver the "donor" car so that the jumper cables will reach both batteries. Turn the donor car off and open both hoods.

1. Connect the black jumper cable to the negative ground terminal of the good car's battery.

2. Connect the other end of the same cable to the negative ground or black terminal of the bad battery.

3. Connect the red cable to the positive terminal of the bad battery.

4. The final connection will be to the (red) positive terminal of the car with the good battery. Doing so will minimize the possibility of a problem with igniting any hydrogen gas that might have been released from the discharged battery, keeping you and your battery safe.

5. Have the car with the good battery start up and put the parking lights on to have a small load on that car's charging system.

6. Go ahead and start the car with the bad battery. It should start right up. Make sure it will stay running and idle.

7. Carefully remove the cables in reverse order.

Frequently Asked Questions

FAQs – Motor Oil

Q) Greg, does the type of engine oil really matter – aren't they all the same?

A) Yes, the oil type matters; and no, the oil types are not all the same. The engine manufacturers call for a specific type and weight of oil to ensure that engine component wear does not exceed a reasonable maximum.

Oil is needed to create a slippery film between the metal parts inside the engine and drive mechanisms to ensure everything slides easily and doesn't scrape together. Think of it as billions of microscopic ball bearings rolling between all the metal parts. They actually keep the parts from touching! Oil's ability to maintain this film is called its "viscosity."

The Society of Automotive Engineers (SAE) has established a numerical code for grading motor oils according to their viscosity. SAE grades include the following, from low to high viscosities: 0, 5, 10,

15, 20, 25, 30, 40, 50 and 60. The numbers 0, 5, 10, 15 and 25 are suffixed with the letter W, designating the "winter" or cold-start viscosity (it doesn't stand for "weight," as many folks think). Essentially, these grades indicate how thick the oil flows when really cold.

Motor oil can be exposed to a wide operating temperature range, from bitter cold on a winter morning before the vehicle starts to very hot when the vehicle is fully warmed up in midsummer heat.

Specific oils will have high viscosity when cold and a lower viscosity at the engine's operating temperature. The difference in viscosities between these temperature extremes is too wide for most single-grade oils to be used year-round.

Additives are used to make the oil *multi-grade* motor oil. The idea is to cause the multi-grade oil to have the viscosity of the base grade when cold and the viscosity of the second grade when hot. This enables one type of oil to be used all year. In fact, when multi-grades were initially developed, they were frequently described as *all-season oil*.

Q) What do those numbers mean?

A) The SAE designation for multi-grade oils includes two viscosity grades; for example, *10W-30* designates common multi-grade oil. The first number '10W' is the viscosity of the oil at cold temperature and the second number is the viscosity at 100 ° Celsius (that's 212 ° Fahrenheit).

Q) Can I change the oil type?

A) Generally, no, it's not a good idea. Stick with what is imprinted on the oil filler cap on top of your engine. Read your owner's manual if you're not sure, or give your shop a call. They'll be able to help.[2]

---

2 Some of this wording is from Wikipedia (http://www.en.wikipedia.com/wiki/Motor_oil).

Q) Can I change the 'brand' of oil?

A) Yes. As far as the oil's ability to perform to minimum standards, 10W-30 from Castrol™ is the same as 10W-30 from Pennzoil™, etc. The API (American Petroleum Institute) designation ('SL' in the image above) is what you should look for on the bottle. This means that the oil has passed the minimum standards to be rated properly.

The different oil manufacturers do have different additive packages and that's how they market their brands. Some additives might make the oil less likely to break down and thus make it last longer. Some might be less apt to burn in older engines, etc.

It's been my philosophy that preventive maintenance and regular oil services go hand in hand. We don't ever want to wait for the oil to fail before replacing it. Engines are just too expensive and oil changes so comparatively inexpensive.

Q) What about 'synthetic' or 'blend' oils?

A) Synthetic oil is specified for more and more modern vehicles. All zero-viscosity oils (0W) are either fully synthetic or a synthetic blend.

Synthetic base-stock lubricant oils are man-made. They are tailored to have a controlled molecular structure with predictable properties. They are composed of organic and inorganic base-stock oils combined with polymer packages to produce synthesized oil compounds.

Semi-synthetic oils are blends of mineral oil with no more than 30% synthetic oil. Sometimes called *synthetic blends,* they are designed to have many of the benefits of synthetic oil without matching the higher cost of pure synthetics.

The primary reason most manufacturers specify pure or blended synthetic oils is to increase fuel economy. It has been reported (although not confirmed) that synthetic oil can increase fuel economy between 2% and 5%. Synthetics do maintain a more stable chemical makeup at low viscosities, which can help reduce engine wear.

The downside of synthetic oil is its cost, which is substantially higher than that of conventional oil.

FAQ – How Often…?

Q) How often to I really NEED to change my oil? Some places say 3,000 miles and some ads say their oil can go 12,000 miles. What's the right thing to do?

A) This mixed message on oil-change frequency is one of my pet peeves… Short answer is, *it depends.* Let me bring our old friend back into the discussion to ask you: how often do you *need* to see your dentist? If you're planning on keeping your set of pearly-whites for the remainder of your days, then I would say "on a regular basis," right?

Preventive maintenance is just that…Pre *(meaning before)* and event *(as in something happening)* …BEFORE SOMETHING HAPPENS. We go to the dentist on a regular basis because, while we may not *like* going, we know that we must go to take care of ourselves; to *prevent* bad things from happening in our teeth. It is the same with our cars. Both can be painful and expensive. All you have to do is to wrap your head around the idea that the *value* of preventing something bad is FAR GREATER than the false savings you might try to use to justify your fear of the dentist's chair – or the repair shop.

Here's the secret that most shops don't pick up on: **WE ARE CREATURES OF HABIT**. *What was that, Greg? What do you mean?*

Well, once we get used to doing something on a regular basis, we know what to expect; we feel much more in control, and our stress levels are much lower.

That's why the best way to maintain your car properly is to have it done in a planned, scheduled, low-stress way on a regular basis.

Most MWI clients drive between 8,000 and 15,000 miles per year, some more, some less. Depending on the year and the model that they drive, we recommend to our clients that we see their car at a regular interval ranging between 3,750 and 5,000 miles, which usually translates to 2 to 4 visits each year.

We modify our suggested schedule to account for the individual client's particular driving habits. The purpose is to maximize their transportation dollars without compromising vehicle life. This is the philosophy that underlies the "SENSIBLE STEWARDS OF YOUR REPAIR DOLLAR" statement in our published corporate mission.

FAQ – Maintenance Minderr

Q) What about the Maintenance Minder? My car tells me when servicing is due.

A) At a training class years ago, a Honda representative informed us that a Maintenance Minder system was going to be integrated into new cars. I knew immediately that this was going to be a big problem; not so much for my business specifically, as for the clients in general. These devices guess at a particular schedule based partially on an individual's driving style. Unfortunately, the day has not yet arrived when an algorithm successfully replaces the experience of a seasoned human service provider.

Since then, at MWI, we've personally witnessed the biggest concern that arose for me way back in that class. If drivers wait

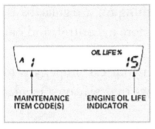

MAINTENANCE ITEM CODE(S)

ENGINE OIL LIFE INDICATOR

until the car tells them that it needs an oil change, it's already overdue.

In one sad case, a client who drove a company-leased Accord scheduled servicing according to the Maintenance Minder. His driving style caused his recommended service intervals to be approximately 12,000 miles apart. Guess what...by the time the car had logged 48,000 miles, the engine was going through excessive quantities of oil—literally burning it. Since the Maintenance Minder system was introduced, we've heard of that situation occurring with increasing frequency. Recently, Honda Motor Company released a service bulletin that actually suggests that service technicians teach all of their clients how to check and add oil to their engines between service stops because it's not unusual for them to run low on oil during the longer maintenance intervals. In my mind, THIS IS RIDICULOUS.

Now, if you're planning on keeping your car for more than 10 years (and I hope you are, as it's the best use of your transportation dollar – more on that later), then it's critical that you prevent major engine problems from occurring 3 to 4 years into ownership, which just so happens to be after the regular warranty from the manufacturer expires. Remember: prevent the event!

Get into the habit of servicing the car on your schedule, in a *proactive* way rather than *reacting* to a guess. The manufacturer stands to gain from you buying a new car; you stand to gain from keeping the one you already paid for in top condition.

Q) Yeah...but wouldn't it be better to just buy a new car? The new ones get better fuel mileage, don't they?

A) The short answers are NO and YES. Stay with me here.

First, consider the environmental impact to the planet of buying a new car.

Cars are made of steel, aluminum, glass, fabrics, chemicals, plastics, and more. Just think of the energy a factory must consume to make a fender or an engine, a steering wheel, a driver seat. It's a substantial amount, and it's hard to grasp; I understand. The car in your driveway has already been built, and no additional energy needs to be expended for those items.

Then there are the environmental, energy, and monetary costs of transporting the car to where you buy it. Sometimes the transit is from only a few states away, and sometimes it means a giant cargo ship traveling across vast oceans:

A 2004 analysis by Toyota Motor Company found that as much as 28% of the carbon dioxide emissions generated during the lifecycle of a typical gasoline-powered car can occur during its manufacture and its transportation to the dealer; the remaining emissions occur during driving once its new owner takes possession. [3]

3 "When Used Cars are More Ecofriendly Than New Cars." *Scientific American* (January 19, 2009): http://www.scientificamerican.com/article/when-used-cars-are-more-ecofriendly/.

Ah…but wait, there's more. What about recycling? Well, all of those components have to go *somewhere* when we junk the car. Just where is '*away*' in our throw-away world? Even if we recycle parts instead of just disposing in landfills, we use quite a bit of energy at quite a cost.

Now, to answer your second question, yes: newer cars do tend to have better fuel economy thanks to breakthroughs in technology and manufacturing methods; but the way you drive also needs to be addressed before you decide to junk your old car. When you sit down and do some math, you might find that the benefit might not exceed the cost; at least, not in our lifetimes.

For example, the fuel-consumption and emission reductions of hybrid models are more than offset by environmental problems posed by the battery and the electric motor they use—at least, in terms of their current technology. Please understand that I believe hybrids are great…it's just that they're not quite cost-effective yet, from either a financial or environmental point of view.

FAQ – Decision to Buy a New Car

Q) What if the repairs needed are more than I think the car is worth?

A) That's a great question—one that, as car owners, we've all probably had to face at one time or another. The first place to look for guidance is your trusted, professional repair shop. If it isn't already part of the maintenance routine, have your shop perform a **Comprehensive Vehicle Inspection.** Similar to getting an annual physical exam at the doctor, this inspection will help you and your shop to determine the overall condition of the car *today*, as well as prospectively. They should be able to guide you with priorities: some things might need to be done now, and others are worth monitoring for a future visit…say 6 months from now.

Once you have a clearer picture of your car's condition, you'll be better informed on how (or whether) to proceed. At my shop, *decisions must be in the client's best interest.* Sometimes, we have to advise a client that this car is just too far gone.

There's more, though. It's not just about the price of the repairs. There is a difference between *price* and *cost*. Let's take a look at the actual costs of buying a new car as compared to repairing the one you already own.

Q) How much does it cost?

A) Many years ago, a client asked me to calculate the lifetime cost of owning a vehicle under long-term maintenance versus frequent new-purchase strategies. I spent a ton of time on this subject. I combed through books, internet sources, and our own data records. Using actual client repair-order data, I created a spreadsheet to determine the customary cost for what the cars actually needed during their lifetimes. I used several Honda models and was quite impressed with the findings.

Before I get to the results, let me quickly describe the components of the **financial costs of ownership:**

1. The purchase price, including

2. Those options *you just* HAD *to have*

3. Sales and/or value-added (ad valorem) taxes. Most states want their cut, too. In Maryland, for example, the sales tax currently is six cents for every dollar, or well over $1000 on a typical new- purchase

4. Title, registration, and tag fees

5. Destination charges (the cost of getting the car to the dealer, almost always passed on to the buyer)

6. Dealer additional costs (otherwise known as overhead, also almost always passed along to the buyer)

7. Increased insurance costs – (yes new cars cost more)

8. Financing – the interest cost you pay to the lender, if you take out a car loan

9. Loss of investment, or what the economists call "opportunity cost" – generally, car purchases make lousy investments (although some classic cars can really provide a nice return). Otherwise, figure this cost as the number of dollars that *your money is NOT making* because you are using it instead to make a car payment every month, when it could have been invested and earning interest or dividends.

10. Initial Depreciation – this is mostly a 'hidden' cost. The car loses more than 20% of its value when you sign the contract in the dealer's office. In that instant, it goes from a 'new' car to a 'used' car. *Twenty percent!* By the end of the 3rd year, the car will have lost almost 40% of its value to depreciation.

11. Annual Depreciation – the amount the car is worth as it becomes another year older. After the steep decline in value in the first three years, the depreciation rate usually settles between 6-8% annually. As the vehicle's age approaches 10 years, the annual depreciation graph flattens out and the value of the car ends up somewhere around 15% of the original purchase price. It is now considered fully depreciated. If the car is still in good

shape, your operating cost per mile should drop significantly! Whoo Hoo!

12. Maintenance and repair costs–This number varies widely with make, model, location, and how you use the vehicle. When I calculated maintenance and repair costs over 12 years of ownership, the daily amount ended up at only **$4.15, which worked out to around $0.10 (yes that's ten cents) per mile.**

Q) What were your results?

A) Somewhat surprising! After careful analysis, my conservative estimates were that

1. Over a 12-year period, it costs **$29,762 more** to trade a car in on a new purchase every 3 years than it does to keep and maintain the same car for 12 years. That works out to $207 in savings per month, every month.

2. Taken a step further… If you invested that monthly savings, then assuming an 8% annual yield,[4] the compounded value of your investment after 144 months (12 years) would balloon to **$49,364.86.**

Recap–you will be saving almost $30,000 PLUS earning a potential $19,364 return on that 30k investment? It sounds fiscally responsible to me.

Now, the decision to purchase a new car isn't always driven by money. There's an *emotional* component too. Acknowledge this…you deserve a new car if you can afford the costs. The message here is to do your due diligence and consider ALL of the

---

4   At the beginning of this subject I mentioned that it was many years ago that I calculated these numbers. At that time, an 8% investment return was conservative. Today's investment returns and current results might vary.

costs, not just the monthly payment. The longer you can keep your car, the less expensive it is to move yourself from point A to point B.

Cars are meant to be driven. Get out and see this fantastic country!

FAQ – Extended Warranties

Q) When I bought my car, the dealership offered me an extended warranty. I didn't buy it but always wondered if it was a smart choice. Was it?

A) Well, I'd have to say you made the smart choice. According to *Consumer Reports*[5], you would be much better off over the life of your car to avoid purchasing the extended warranty. Many people forget they even bought the warranty by the time they may need it!

There are several reasons why it's usually wiser to decline the extended warranty. I'll limit the discussion to four of them.

---

5 Consumer Reports. "Don't Buy Extended Warranties: You'd Be Smarter to Set Aside the Money You'd Spend to Cover Repair Costs Yourself."
https://www.consumerreports.org/shopping/dont-buy-extended-warranties/

First: An extended warranty is basically an insurance policy. Insurance is not necessarily a bad thing, but it depends on what you're insuring against, and how much it costs. Understand that with extended warranties, *for-profit* corporations have created a tool to collect premiums and pay claims. Insurance is profitable because, even though a few insured people will one day collect very large individual claims, the overwhelming majority of insured people pay far more in premiums than they will ever collect in claims. For an individual, it's worth taking that loss to insure against certain types of risk in one's life for which the cost would be catastrophic; but to insure against the possibility of only *some kinds* of auto repairs, the probable costs—relative to the potential benefit—are very high.

Second: The deductible. In my opinion, there are really two deductibles. The first one of course is the dollar amount you'll be responsible for after the repair. The second? That's the time you must spend getting the dealer, or automaker, or whoever sold you the insurance policy, to do what they said (or what you understood) they were going to do. All the claims person has to do is say 'no' and…bingo… this is how it starts. How much is your time worth? We only get 24 hours every day and I certainly don't want to waste mine trying to pry enough money for new parts from some guy in another part of the country, or the world, for that matter.

Third: Statistically, you're almost certain to be one of those people noted above who provide the profit margin for the insurer. That means you'll likely never get your money back out of the premiums that they rolled into your car payment. By the way, if you financed your purchase, you are paying interest on that premium too. Ouch.

 **Finally**: there are many items that extended warranties do not cover. The ads or brochures don't talk about this much and…surprise…they don't cover any test-

ing, fluids, most of the seals, etc. The warranties usually stipulate flat amounts they will pay for certain items regardless of how much the repair shop charges. These differences are sometimes passed right back to you. File this under "read the fine print." If you are still sold on paying for the policy, that's okay, just ask to read the exclusions section beforehand.

Here's a good one for you. Consider taking the cost of the extended warranty that you were considering and put it instead into a separate bank account. You'll most likely always have enough money in the account for occasional repairs. That can help lessen any unexpected expense stress.

Q) But what if I DID buy one of these? How should I handle it?

A) No worries. Gather up all the information you have on the warranty and the insurer and bring it to your shop's Service Advisor. He or she will review what you have, make copies as necessary and, at least in the case of MWI, contact the insurance company on your behalf to work through the claim. We have a pretty good track record with most of them and have experienced (and very patient) professionals going to bat for you.

FAQ – Motor Clubs

Q) How beneficial are motor club memberships?

A) Motor clubs provide good benefits, and offer peace of mind for the consumer who travels a lot. Undoubtedly, their primary focus is the customer. I am thinking of clubs like AAA Motor Club or Cross Country Motor Club, the two big wheels in the industry.

It's easy to feel vulnerable when traveling through an unfamiliar part of the country. These clubs help locate a reliable repair facility, a towing company, a hotel, and other things of that nature. Therefore, you have more confidence in the quality of service you will receive.

Some car insurance policies and credit cards offer many of these benefits automatically at no additional cost. Take some time to review the features section of each. I happen to be a long-term member of the American Motorcycling Association and it turns out they offer a road-service benefit as well. They even extend coverage to any automobile in my family. Knock on wood, I haven't used it yet and hope not to.

FAQ – Gasoline

Q) Do I need to buy premium fuel?

A) The best way to determine if premium fuel is right for you is to check your owner's manual. Higher performance vehicles will usually require premium fuel. In most cases, the fuel gauge itself will indicate if premium fuel is required.

Let's understand the differences between regular and premium fuel. Please know that all gasoline is pretty much the same chemically. The premium fuels include an additive package and have a higher *"octane"* rating.

The higher the octane rating, the more the fuel burns at a controlled rate inside the engine rather than having a mini-explosion going on inside there. The controlled expansion of the burning gasses creates an even pressure on the tops of the pistons and therefore will be more efficient, extracting the maximum amount of power from the fuel.

Alternatively, when the fuel explodes rather than burning at a controlled rate, a tremendous amount of pressure builds for a very short time on the top of each piston. These explosions are called *"knocks"* or *"pings"*. This condition causes excessive heat inside the combustion area, poor power output, and bad emissions; it can be really bad for the engine overall.

Modern cars use knock sensors; when they detect these explosions, they signal the ECU (engine control unit) to de-tune the engine until it the pinging stops. Although that addresses the pinging problem, the result is a more sluggish car that gets fewer miles per gallon of gas.

FAQ – Certification

Q) What is ASE and why is it important?

ASE = Automotive Service Excellence

You'll see this one a lot. Shortened from the original **National Institute for Automotive Service Excellence**, ASE is an independent, non-profit organization that tests the competency of those working in our industry. ASE does not provide training; it only evaluates competency. Testing is administered with a proctor just the same as a student taking the ACT or SAT exam.

There are eight standard categories of ASE certification. When a Technician is certified in all eight, he or she is awarded Master Technician certification.

Technicians can qualify for ASE advanced certification in gas- or diesel-powered cars and trucks. ASE also certifies parts vendors and service consultants.

ASE is the "gold standard" in our industry, and in my opinion, it is critical that anyone who works on your vehicle should be an ASE Certified Technician. Before you have any work done on your vehicle, look for or ask to see their credentials. While certification is voluntary, a repair shop that displays its ASE certificates takes pride in staying ahead of the curve and signals additional credibility to motorists choosing a repair provider. ASE certification must be renewed periodically, which ensures that your shop stays on top of the technological changes required to service newer vehicles properly and professionally.

Conclusion

I would like to thank all of you for taking the time to read this book. I must say, the time it took was more than six times what I expected. I found the process almost cathartic in a way. I know there were lessons I needed to learn from this process and I am grateful for the opportunity.

I would ask you to consider giving this book to a friend, child or other family member. You can purchase them from Amazon.com or through the Motor Works, Inc. Just contact us at 301-424-2800 and we'll make it so.

The references in this book certainly could help when out in your car. I would suggest putting a copy in the glove compartment.

For up to date information and new articles, please visit www.motor-works.com where you can set vehicle appointments, learn about your car and read blog posts. You can like us on Facebook (*www.facebook.com/motorworksinc*) and subscribe to up to the minute Tweets on Twitter (*@motorworksinc*) or view some informative videos on our YouTube channel (*MotorWorksInc*).

About the Author

G reg Skolnik, Owner, Director, and Master Technician, has guided the shop from its inception to the well-established and highly regarded service facility it is today. A 1974 graduate of Lincoln Technical Institute with a degree in Automotive Technology, He is certified as a Master Automobile Technician and holds the prestigious L-1 advanced engine performance and emission analysis certification. In November of 2004, Greg also received the coveted Accredited Auto-motive Management (A.A.M.) degree  and in March of 2017, received an Accredited Masters degree (A.M.A.M.) from the Automotive Management Institute.

Greg gives back to the industry and helps others by working as a Business Development Coach for other auto shops around the country. See www.eliteworldwide.com

Greg and his wife Carol have two grown sons. Their older son, Chris and his wife Mary gave birth to Joshua in July of 2009. Their younger son, Aaron gave them three beautiful grandchildren: Kayleigh in September of 1999; Nathan in August of 2003; and Olivia in April of 2008. "Pop Pop" and "Nana" continue to practice spoiling all four.

Greg is still a Scout Leader with more than 30 years with Boy Scout Troop and Venturing Crew 1083 in Rockville, Maryland and finally figured out how to tie all those knots! Greg also enjoys touring on his motorcycle and still plays his drums for fun.

Made in the USA
Columbia, SC
02 July 2018